# THE FACE OF POETRY

First credited portrait of a poet by LaVerne Harrell Clark to be published in a national magazine. Robert Peter Tristram Coffin, as he appeared in 1950. Photo published in *American Scandinavian Review* (June, Summer, 1951, Volume XXXIX, #2, p. 161), credited under maiden name of photographer.

Dedicated to *so* many:

L.D. Clark, my favorite novelist, and to Mother and Dolly, too, because they helped him buy me my first camera during those lean Columbia University days of ours . . .

the late Boyce Harrell, Daddy, who helped with the camera, too, and who taught me my first poem besides . . .

the late Robert P. Tristram Coffin, my first poet friend at TWU, and subject of my first credited magazine portrait . . .

the late Ruth Stephan, poet-novelist and friend, who first envisioned, endowed, and helped to found what is now the University of Arizona Poetry Center.

And to all my good poet friends, both in this book and others along the trail, but especially to Richard Eberhart and Donald Hall for constant encouragement and support, and to my warm buddies of many years, "the Fieries and the Snuffies" of the Tucson Corral—Richard and Lois Shelton, Phyllis Gibbs, Peter Wild, Robert Longoni, etc. . . . Heck, you *know* your brand . . .

Know now my gratitude,

LaVerne Harrell Clark

*For the Library of the College of Marin*
*In Loving Memory of*
*Grazia Patricia (Johnson) Youan,*
*Who attended Your College—*
*With remembrance of her cousin,*

# THE FACE OF POETRY:
## 101 Poets In Two Significant Decades
## —the 60's & the 70's

Photographic portraits by
LaVerne Harrell Clark

*LaVerne Harrell*
*Clark*

Foreword by
Richard Eberhart

*Tucson, Az*
*Jan. 4, 1992.*

Edited by
LaVerne Harrell Clark
and
Mary MacArthur

Heidelberg Graphics · Chico, Ca. · 1979

First published, 1977 by Gallimaufry Press (ISBN 0-916300-07-2)
Second Printing, 1979 by Heidelberg Graphics (ISBN 0-918606-04-7)
Printed in the U.S.A.

Library of Congress Cataloging in Publication Data
Clark, LaVerne Harrell.
    The face of poetry.

    Reprint of the ed. published by Gallimaufry, Arling-
ton, Va.
    1. Poetry, Modern—20th century.    2. Poets—20th
century—Portraits.    I. MacArthur, Mary.    II. Title.
PN6101.C59    1979        808.81'046        79-17351
ISBN 0-918606-04-7

Heidelberg Graphics' publications are available direct from Post
Office Box 3606, Chico, California 95927, or from other distributors
and library jobbers.

# ACKNOWLEDGMENTS

Some of the photographic portraits in this volume first appeared in the following publications: *Sumac, Great Lakes Review, Poetry Now, Coda: Poets & Writers Newsletter, Windless Orchard, Pembroke, The Poetry Society of America: Bulletin, Amotfa, The Round Up: Official Organ of the Western Writers of America,* and David Allan Evans' *New Voices in American Poetry* (Winthrop Publishers, Cambridge, Massachusetts, 1973).

For permission to use some of the selections in this volume, grateful acknowledgment is made to the following poets and executors:

Randall Ackley for FOR A YOUNG WOMAN LYING ALONE IN BED, copyright © 1976 by Randall Ackley.

Paula Gunn Allen for THE TRICK IS CONSCIOUSNESS, copyright © 1976 by Paula Gunn Allen.

Leonard Bird for WALTER MITTY, copyright © 1976 by Leonard Bird.

Thomas Cobb for BERTRAM DECLINES, copyright © 1976 by Thomas Cobb.

Victor Hernández Cruz for THE FOUR CORNERS, copyright © 1976 by Victor Hernández Cruz.

Michael Cuddihy for MY HOUSE, copyright © 1976 by Michael Cuddihy.

Richard Eberhart for TIME'S OFFERINGS, copyright © 1976 by Richard Eberhart.

Dan Gerber for A FINE EXCESS, copyright © 1976 by Dan Gerber.

Miguel González-Gerth for TRAGICOMIC CONCEIT, copyright © 1976 by Miguel González-Gerth.

Drummond Hadley for SPRINGTIME, copyright © 1976 by Drummond Hadley.

Michael S. Harper for GRANDFATHER, copyright © 1976 by Michael S. Harper.

Jim Harrison for JIM—AGE 38, 5′ 10″, W. 196, STRAPPING GOGGLE-EYED NORDIC BANKRUPT, copyright © 1976 by Jim Harrison.

Lawson Fusao Inada for CAPTION, CIRCA 1972, copyright © 1976 by Lawson Fusao Inada.

Jeremy Ingalls for TRAITS: INNER PORTRAIT, copyright © 1976 by Jeremy Ingalls.

Will Inman for LATE ADVISORY FOR INTERGALACTIC TRAVELLERS SUCH AS POETS, copyright © 1976 by Will Inman.

June Jordan for UNTITLED, from *These Poems,* copyright © 1974 by June Jordan.

Carolyn Maisel for Part XII from PIG WOMAN, copyright © 1976 by Carolyn Maisel.

Howard McCord for JENNIFER, copyright © 1976 by Howard McCord.

Carol S. Merrill for PORTRAIT, copyright © 1976 by Carol S. Merrill.

Susan North for RUMOR YOU CALLED MY NAME, copyright © 1976 by Susan North.

Steve Orlen for NO QUARTER, copyright © 1976 by Steve Orlen.

Simon J. Ortiz for MORNING SMALLFIRE IN LUKACHUKAI MOUNTAINS, copyright © 1975 by Simon J. Ortiz.

Grateful acknowledgement for the second printing of this book is made to the original publisher and co-editor, Mary MacArthur of Gallimaufry Press which has temporarily suspended publication, for her cooperation and assistance, and to Larry S. Jackson of Heidelberg Graphics, from LaVerne Harrell Clark, photographer and co-editor, who realizes that without their belief this book would not be here.

Mrs. Clark wishes to further acknowledge with deepest gratitude the gracious and continued help of Ms. Lois Olsrud, Humanities Reference Librarian, and the entire staff of both the Humanities and the Main Library of the University of Arizona, Tucson.

# FOREWORD

LaVerne Clark has a sprightly idea which is to show the best and characteristic pictures of many shots of poets she has taken over the last ten years. This book has a warm human interest, delights us with a casual, non-formal approach to her subjects so that the viewer may, in fact, see what the poets look like, off-hand, when they were not posing.

Americans may read poetry for years without seeing pictures of the poets. Quite a number of anthologists, of whom the first I recall was Oscar Williams, published pictures of poets along with their poems, which heightened the interest of such volumes. In this case, it is the pictures alone (plus one poem) so that the readers of each poet may enjoy a new look of their man or woman, or may be intrigued to read the work of some poet they now see for the first time.

The poets in this book are young, or old, and some are now dead, increasing the value of LaVerne Clark's photographs of them a while ago.

It is a fascinating subject. Most historical poets are known by perhaps only one set picture and before our times only by portraits or drawings. I recall for decades only one picture of Hardy, stiff, formal, impersonal, without feeling. I saw a picture of John Donne a year ago ornately dressed, as elaborately tricked out as Queen Elizabeth. How interesting if we had off-hand, informal depictions of these. How did Milton look when walking in London? What did Blake really look like, or Keats, or Shelley, or Byron? How did Hopkins look when teaching a class? I never felt very close to any of the old historical poets from seeing their formal depictions, but now in this century a photographer can increase a reader's interest by doing what LaVerne Clark does so well in this focus on the chance moment, a special moment of being.

I am grateful to her for snapping her quick shutter in each case in this attractive book, allowing a social hour to the viewers.

—Richard Eberhart

# CONTENTS

The dates in parentheses beneath the photographic portraits
indicate when the photographs were taken.

# THE FACE OF POETRY:

# Randall Ackley
(June 1975)

# FOR A YOUNG WOMAN LYING ALONE IN BED

The old troll,
With his black bag of
Bad dreams, a shark's tooth, lies,
Poetry, a bear's claw,
Wishes he carried the cock
Of a three year old stallion,
Bore the heart of an eagle,
Soaring high, mating in the eyes of the Sun,
Challenging Apollo and his stallions;
And insatiable Venus-Aphrodite, too,
To a game of Love.

He would drink the great horn dry,
With its tip in the Sea;
Then
Begin the creation of a race of Giant
Troll-gods.

He would conceive a sun
Each moment,
Peopling this entire cosmos
With the fruits of his loins,
His heart, his love.

But he wanders on,
With his black bag,
His bad dreams, his lies, his poetry,
His boots, symbolic of his lusts,
But carrying him only as a
Weary Pied Piper,
With flapping trouser legs,
Flags of his defeats.

# Paula Gunn Allen

(June 1975)

# THE TRICK IS CONSCIOUSNESS

Mistaken.
take.    en.
mis      t.
mind
it might as well as
though understandings were
babies
suppers
sheep
winding sheets
roads
the twists
grimace of time.
temporality.
sense
ation.
(the waves, swells, riding) dur
ation.
do you remember the light.
I think about long ago
(as they say, or said, *humma ho*)
and wonder how the earth has changed
not I but
it in twenty years, wonder at
the completeness of it,
gone somewhere down roads, sheets, twists of days,
getting, forgetting, sudden realization, no
excuses, no surmise,
there it is.

I remember the corral behind the house,
the wooden stairs up to it, chicken house, stall, rabbit pen,
pigeon pen, the high ricks shading.
It was full during the war.  My father
didn't want us to want—there were chickens, rabbits, a cow

that gave enough for the whole village, sheep, pigeons, a huge pig.
They made chicherones when they slaughtered it.
I was maybe four.
Later the corral was empty.
Used to wander around in it, wondering.
I still do, at night, at dream.
And I remember grandma's mulch bed—
the crazy lily pond she ran us out of,
the tamarack tree behind the coal shed, deep
shadows there, spider webs, trumpet vine, I
dream about them now, sound, smell, shade and light
so complete—I have changed nothing.

The key is in remembering, in what is chosen for the dream.
In the silence of recovery we hold
the rituals of the dawn,
now as then.

Watch.

The cycle grows impassable.
To be beholden.
Uncomprehending but beheld.
I think of dawn in July, watched from the mesa behind my house,
the still purple village groping toward light,
sky on fire
not in metaphor
clouds billows of smoke:
I didn't know then what it signified, but I watched,
still,
shivering in the quick cold air.  I was twelve.
In full daylight the mountains were pale,
the long sunbitten afternoons
were and still are uncomprehended in their completeness,
consummate wish somehow buried
in the space of time passing
gone before our eyes, that yesterday.
Nobody goes down the old highway in wagons anymore.
But they did.

Wind in early morning, June, the perfect smell of clarity.
Did you know that the trees were gold then,
the light was, no explanation for it, but there it was.
The free air coming in the window.
Trick of sunlight? Trick of eyes?
It doesn't do that anymore. No tricks this time.
The trees showered light like clouds shower water.
Four summers or more it was that way, all
the times I woke in summer. No matter what
color my room was painted.
It was like that since I was a baby.
So there is that.
Childhood holds such mystery. I live it over and over—
at night, in sleep, during the day,
watching,
waking.
Those trees were mystery.
When you looked you knew they were green,
though your mind held gold, holds it still.
Behind them stood the sky, silent accomplice to their will.

The bark was rough and silvery.
Grandma didn't like those Chinese elm trees, I
couldn't understand why. We would sit lazy crooked in the branches,
chattering through long afternoons, trying to read the clouds.
How could we know then what is so plain to us now?

Control is out of reach.
We knew that then.
As now we know that outside these lighted islands of our lives
the dark is growing
hurtling toward us at the speed of light.

# Jon Anderson
(February 1972)

# YEARS

Sometimes in weariness I stop.
Because I've been lucky
I think the future must be plain.
Over the trees the stars are quite small.

My friends talk quietly
& we have all come to the same things.
Now if I die, I will
Inherit awhile their similar bodies.

Now if I listen
Someone is telling a story.
The characters met.
They enchanted each other by speech.

Though the stories they lived
Were not the same,
Many were distracted into love,
Slept, & woke alone, awhile serene.

# Marvin Bell

(February 1972)

# TRINKET

I love watching the water
ooze through the crack in the fern pot,
it's a small thing

that slows time
and steadies
and gives me ideas of becoming

having nothing to do
with ambition or even reaching,
it isn't necessary at such times

to describe this,
it's no image for mean keeping,
it's no thing that small

but presence.
Other men look at the ocean,
and I do too,

though it is too many
presences for any
to absorb.

It's this other,
a little water, used, appearing
slowly around the sounds

of oxygen and small frictions,
that gives the self
the notion of the self

one is always losing
until these tiny embodiments
small enough to contain it.

# Leonard Bird

(June 1975)

# WALTER MITTY

I dream of making love
slowly    often    and well
to all the lovely women of the world
kissing every breast and thigh
touching with my wicked tongue
the incense of a thousand anxious lips.

I dream of writing great sheaves of poems
to fan the coals of sensual memory
to reconnect the silken thread
and guide us through the silence of the maze.

I dream of leading one courageous war
within the swamps and forests of the soul
of breaking through enchanted walls
to free the prisoners of fear.

But in the glare of morning light
I sweat to write one crooked line
sip my cup of sugared tea
and stretch to touch your hand.

# Louise Bogan

(February 1967)
deceased

# SONNET

Since you would claim the sources of my thought
Recall the meshes whence it sprang unlimed,
The reedy traps which other hands have timed
To close upon it. Conjure up the hot
Blaze that it cleared so cleanly, or the snow
Devised to strike it down. It will be free.
Whatever nets draw in to prison me
At length your eyes must turn to watch it go.

My mouth, perhaps, may learn one thing too well,
My body hear no echo save its own,
Yet will the desperate mind, maddened and proud,
Seek out the storm, escape the bitter spell
That we obey, strain to the wind, be thrown
Straight to its freedom in the thunderous cloud.

# George Bowering
(November 1963)

The crusht cigar, a
   "sadism" of your last
      night, cigars, the
         sexual machine. He
      tries totemic figures. He
         tries Cain, he is a
         butterfly, a snake, where
you have gone is the green
         flame, oh, that's frame, of
            death, a


cigar, an emblem in the heavens,
      Where have you,
         you, gone.
                     What have you
            What have I, Black humorist,
to do with it, a classical satyr


   ashamed of his love, a
Villon,    these names, what


   name have you, a
   cigar I stub, faecal
   image, naive boy.

# Bobby Byrd

## (May 1975)

# LET ME FOR ONCE

Let me for once
speak of the fool
that resides in
this house I give
my name to—this
stack of bones &
muscle, this heart,
this mind, this
unholy one who says
so easily he will
have all these
worlds offered, will
speak of God, of
the wobbley-legged
dance in sunshine,
in moonshine, in
the shine of a woman's
legs, in the hell
of what he came for,
the hole born from
his mother's womb,
the constant choice
of who he is, the
blessing of his work.
This fool I speak of,
his easy way, his
laughter, the one
I search for, drink with,
the God-damned way
of his life, his unholy
way of worship:
I can say no more.

# Jefferson Carter
(June 1976)

# HOW TO WRITE A POEM ABOUT THE DESERT

I grew up
in these blond
mottled foothills
under the profile
of a man sleeping
on his back.
Spun my horse, bareback,
after jackrabbits
the color of smoke
whose donkey ears
periscoped for danger.
Smelled the thin odor
of creosote after rain,
that blade
in the dark washed air.
I didn't love
the desert;
it was there,
the distance
between shadows,
the reluctant shade
of the Palo Verde trees,
an arroyo leading
away. I've come back
looking for subjects,
not love.

# John Ciardi
(March 1971)

# WASHING YOUR FEET

Washing your feet is hard when you get fat.

     *       *       *

In lither times the act was unstrained and pleasurable.

     *       *       *

You spread the toes for signs of athlete's foot.

     *       *       *

You used creams, and rubbing alcohol, and you powdered.

     *       *       *

You bent over, all in order, and did everything.

     *       *       *

Mary Magdelene made a prayer meeting of it.

     *       *       *

She, of course, was washing not her feet but God's.

     *       *       *

Degas painted ladies washing their own feet.

     *       *       *

Somehow they also seem to be washing God's feet.

     *       *       *

To touch any body anywhere should be ritual.

     *       *       *

To touch one's own body anywhere should be ritual.

     *       *       *

Fat makes the ritual wheezy and a bit ridiculous.

     *       *       *

Ritual and its idea should breathe easy.

     *       *       *

They are memorial, meditative, immortal.

     *       *       *

Toenails keep growing after one is dead.

     *       *       *

Washing my feet, I think of immortal toenails.

     *       *       *

What are they doing on these ten crimped polyps?

     *       *       *

I reach to wash them and begin to wheeze.

     *       *       *

I wish I could paint like Degas or believe like Mary.

     *       *       *

It is sad to be naked and to lack talent.

     *       *       *

It is sad to be fat and to have dirty feet.

# Neil Claremon

(January 1970)

# HALF-YEAR BIRTHDAY

I can't move I stand upwind and still,
the coyote drinks at a leaking pipe
shrill laughter of a pack
echoing off last night;
I know that space turns on itself,
a wild dog
30 ft from our porch is an entrance
to a cryptic animal world, but
my leg's so bruised I haul it with me
hot day after day!
When she turns she holds me fixed
in her black and white frame—
at this moment of congruence
we stand in fear of traps and poisons
protecting ourselves with daylight—
now she limps toward me
as if I weren't here, a body
for a moment outside time,
and holds her pace to the chaparral
a gift I had.
I am 32 and a half; lame as the coyote
I know the others would kill her.

Lucille Clifton

(November 1975)

# UNTITLED

the thirty eighth year
of my life,
plain as bread
round as a cake
an ordinary woman.

an ordinary woman.

i had expected to be
smaller than this,
more beautiful,
wiser in Afrikan ways,
more confident,
i had expected
more than this.

i will be forty soon.
my mother once was forty.

my mother died at forty-four,
a woman of sad countenance
leaving behind a girl
awkward as a stork.
my mother was thick,
her hair was a jungle and
she was very wise
and beautiful
and sad.

i have dreamed dreams
for you mama
more than once.
i have wrapped me
in your skin
and made you live again

more than once.
i have taken the bones you hardened
and built daughters
and they blossom and promise fruit
like Afrikan trees.
i am a woman now.
an ordinary woman.

in the thirty eighth
year of my life,
surrounded by life,
a perfect picture of
blackness blessed,
i had not expected this
loneliness.

if it is western,
if it is the final
Europe of my mind,
if in the middle of my life
i am turning the final turn
into the shining dark
let me come to it whole
and holy
not afraid
not lonely
out of my mother's life
into my own.
into my own.

i had expected more than this.
i had not expected to be
an ordinary woman.

# Thomas Cobb
(June 1976)

# BERTRAM DECLINES

*for Leon Peterson*

Bertram fingers the sweat
from his glasses, replaces them
and pulls the world back into his head.
"Hotter than a sixteen-year-old
schoolgirl, ain't it?

Now I appreciate your offer,
but you spend the summer
on that mountain by yourself.
I feel no kin with mountains,
never have.  That green music
requires a dancing I can't do.
In forests you can't look
at just one tree.  No,
I'm at home on the desert,
content with small shade.
The beauty of the desert is easy;
each thing stands out
like the good deeds of a man,
more beautiful for being few."

# Robert J. Conley
(June 1976)

# SELF-PORTRAIT:
## MICROCOSM, OR, SONG OF MIXED-BLOOD

### 1.

In me the Cherokee
wars against *unega* (white)
I have college degrees (2)
all major credit cards
pay my bills on time each month
on my wall is a photograph
of the Great Spirit

### 2.

Because the meat I eat
comes wrapped in cellophane
I do not understand
the first facts of life

I have never drunk blood
and I hunt
with the channel selector
in front of my tv

### 3.

When I go to the supermarket
and buy some meat
pre-cut and wrapped
how do I apologize
to the spirit of the animal
whose meat I eat
and where shall I build my fires?

4.

My poems are my fires.
oh gods forgive me all
the things I've failed
to do.  the things I should
have done.  forgive the meat
I've used without a prayer
without apology forgive
the other prayers I haven't
said those times I should
but oh ye gods both great
and small I do not know
the ancient forms.  my poems
are my fires and my prayers.

# Robert Creeley
## (December 1963)

# LUNCH AND AFTER

I don't want to leave
so quickly, the lovely

faces, surrounding, human
terms so attractive. And

the world, the *world*, we
could think of, *here,* to-

gether, a flash of instant, a
million years of time.

Don't, myself, be an
old man yet, I want to

move out and into this
physical, endless place.

Sun's dazzling shine now
back of the towering clouds,

and sounds of builders'
pounding, faint, distant

buzz of traffic. Mirror's
in front of me, hat's on

head, under it, human
face, my face, reddened,

it seems, lined, grey's
in beard and mustache—

not only *myself* but an-
other man has got to

at last walk out and into
another existence, out there,

that haze that softens those trees,
all those other days to come.

(Kuala Lumpur—April 15,1976)

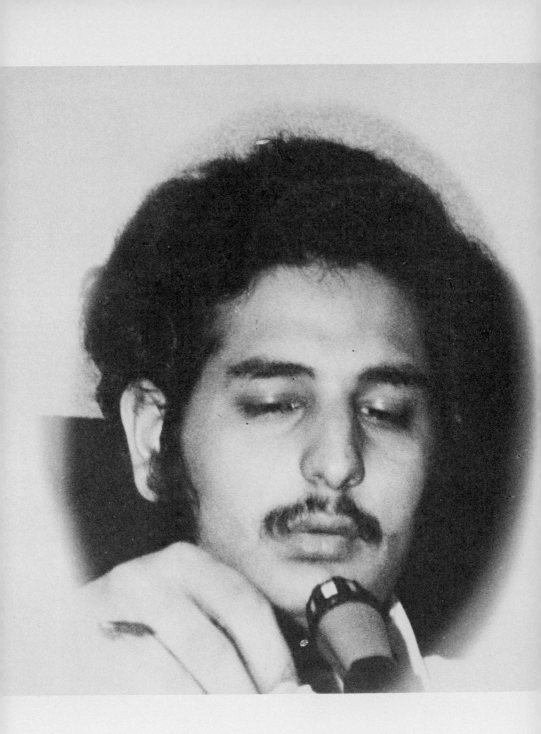

# Victor Hernández Cruz
### (November 1971)

# THE FOUR CORNERS

The first corner has become a
bodega whose window is full of
Platanos who have traveled the
Miles to rest in that reality
Green with splashes of black
running down their spines
The other corner had a restaurant
A crab running out the door
Speaking: You can't write about
my belly unless you taste it
The other third corner found
a group of friends singing
They become clocks with their:
A zoon zoon zoon
Zoon su Babare
The last and final corner
is where I stand
Like a sucker making this up.

# Michael Cuddihy
(May 1976)

# MY HOUSE

The east wall's so white.
An ice cube—
Something inside melting it.
The full moon maybe,
Drifting south over the airbase.

I can feel it on my skin.
All around me the neighbors' lights
Go out.

There, in the white spaces between the salt cedars
To see yourself,
The wind in the hair-like clusters, needles
Like lungs opening and closing.

This door,
I have to lean all my weight against it.

If I really wanted to
Nights like this, I could walk out, leaving
My body behind
Like a birdhouse
The rains have rotted
Until it is fallen in on itself,
The wood around the nails rusty—

A few sunflower seeds
In case somebody's hungry in the morning.

# C.Day Lewis

(April 1965)
deceased

# THE GATE

### *for Trekkie*

In the foreground, clots of cream-white flowers (meadow-
    sweet?
Guelder? Cow parsley?): a patch of green: then a gate
Dividing the green from a brown field; and beyond,
By steps of mustard and sainfoin-pink, the distance
Climbs right-handed away
Up to an olive hilltop and the sky.

The gate it is, dead-centre, ghost-amethyst-hued,
Fastens the whole together like a brooch.
It is all arranged, all there, for the gate's sake
Or for what may come through the gate. But those white
    flowers,
Craning their necks, putting their heads together,
Like a crowd that holds itself back from surging forward,
Have their own point of balance—poised, it seems,
On the airy brink of whatever it is they await.

And I, gazing over their heads from outside the picture,
Question what we are waiting for: not summer—
Summer is here in charlock, grass and sainfoin.
A human event?—but there's no path to the gate,
Nor does it look as if it was meant to open.
The ghost of one who often came this way
When there was a path? I do not know. But I think,
If I could go deep into the heart of the picture

From the flowers' point of view, all I would ask is
Not that the gate should open, but that it should
Stay there, holding the coloured folds together.
We expect nothing (the flowers might add), we only
Await: this pure awaiting—
It is the kind of worship we are taught.

" 'The Gate' was inspired by a landscape which I bought for him [C. Day Lewis]
when I could see that he was drawn to it like a magnet. We were staying with the
artist (to whom the poem was dedicated), and it's a poem about the nature of
religion—or—if you like—inspiration and the awaiting."

—Mrs. C. Day Lewis

# Abelardo Delgado

(June 1975)

# MY STAR SPANGLED-RED STRIPED SOCKS

what will i do next?
when will my ego rest?
full beard . . running
                    on a track suit,
another fast?
              wear my bright poncho
                              on the plane?
shave my head?  wear a silly hat?
wear my star spangled-red striped socks?
add a new news story
                 in which my name appears
to my old scrap book?
recite a poem at a wedding,
in a funeral? give a rap
in a school or college?
confront the establishment?
this manic or maniac
upmanship
              must certainly have
a why or a few of them
                    behind,
a lonely, fear-full aging man
drawing unto him
the necessary attention
not to ego-trip
but to die quietly
                 in the superficial glory of
—that was good, lalo.—
even my fantasies of greatness
are mediocre
              and so common
as i truly yearn to be.
i lose myself among my brother freaks.
i suffer so . . . to get my kicks.

# R.P. Dickey
(February 1976)

# ANOTHER VIEW OF THE BEAST

He's seldom the way anybody wants
him to be.  Not to disturb, not
to disturb.  To get work done
in time before he's ushered out of it.
From a deliberate center
of idiosyncratic arbitrariness,
he acts.  Contrary to you,
and to most of himself.

"Oh I appreciate individuality
as much as the next person, but why
would anyone want to do *that?*"
you will say as he stands out of sight
smiling up the sleeve of some
unfashionable shirt which doesn't fit
him as it should—and what is he doing
wearing it on a night like this?

It's a hot night and he wants to be
inside, no air conditioning, buttoned up
inside a Navy peacoat, for God's sake.
His problem is that he has driven you
away from him, pretty much, and labors
away at a new work, driving his doubts
out of the house with the clatter
of the keys, putting up with himself,
wondering, between sheets, what you
are really up to, hassling synonymies, heading
for the refrigerator he knows is out of beer.

He opens it and looks inside anyhow.
He's too much for television,
doesn't own a set, is just now
busy re-reading *Othello* yet again,
so perfect it makes him want to quit
and give more time to his son, quit
and give more time to making
the proper connections for jobs,
politics, thin out into *it.*  Quit.

Why doesn't he? All the dumb bulk
he's piling up anyway! He's been asked
to leave town; but his passel of manuscripts
grows so unluggable he would need three trucks;
and besides, he likes it where he is.

Norman Dubie

(January 1976)

## ABOUT INFINITY: A SELF-PORTRAIT,
## BUT NOT OF THE BODY WHICH WILL BE CARTED AWAY!

*To Matisse.*

There are stone breakers in straw hats
Drinking from jars under a shade tree.
You are dressed all in white like the clematis
And look down into a meadow where your father
Is working on a watercolor of two silver trees.
The two trees are parallel.
He looks back at you:
You are wishing he hadn't died making with
His chest a sound like cows running in a stream.

Cows eat the flowers, they eat off the trees;
And the seed packets of the milk-white clematis
Have no turnings: they sit, almost purple,
In steady needles that are all vertical, North
And South, repeating abstractly
That such parallel things must meet
Somewhere in a limitless glut of peace.

There are men in straw hats drinking from clear
Jars of water.
There are two silver trees whose pink roots
Will meet, not abstractly, but under the meadow
Where for minerals and the water
They mean to kill one another. There are cows

Running in a running stream.

## Alan Dugan

### (December 1966)

# UNTITLED POEM

I've promised that I will not care about things,
persons, or myself, but I do. For example:
my house looks like a set for a New England tragedy
but it isn't. Outside it looks like a dump.
What it's like inside I'm too arrogant to describe
although we're happy for whole moments at a time
during this ''life is pain'' phenomenon.
Nevertheless my objects, loves and self
interfere with my own being. We should,
me and my wife, burn all this down
and start again possessionless toward death
and not together, which is nonsense. Loves,
marriages, families are stultifying in
accumulations of debris of love and artifacts.
Let it all go, as it will, upwards in the fire after death.

# Stephen Dunn
(December 1975)

# BIOGRAPHY IN THE FIRST PERSON

This is not the way I am.
Really, I am much taller in person,
the hairline I conceal reaches back
to my grandfather, and the shyness my wife
will not believe in has always been why
I was bold on first dates. All my uncles
were detectives. My father a crack salesman.
I've saved his pins, the small acclamations
I used to show my friends. And the billyclub
I keep by my bed was his, too; an heirloom.
I am somewhat older than you can tell.
The early deaths have decomposed
behind my eyes, leaving lines apparently caused
by smiling. My voice still reflects the time
I believed in prayer as a way of getting
what I wanted. I am none of my clothes.
My poems are approximately true.
The games I play and how I play them
are the arrows you should follow: they'll take you
to the enormous body of a child. It is not
that simple. At parties I have been known to remove
from the bookshelf the kind of book
that goes best with my beard.
My habits in bed are so perverse they differentiate me
from no one. And I prefer soda, the bubbles just after
it's opened, to anyone who just lies there. Be careful:
I would like to make you believe in me.
When I come home at night after teaching myself
to students, I want to search the phone book
for their numbers, call them, and pick their brains.
Oh, I am much less flamboyant than this.
If you ever meet me, I'll be the one with the lapel
    full of carnations.

# Richard Eberhart

(March 1972)

# TIME'S OFFERINGS

Twenty years ago it seemed the same.
The view of paradise visible to the eye
Paradisiacal then, is paradisiacal now.
What has changed? The sky a bright blue of May,
The flowers all out in an orderly array,
The river, which cracked with ice breaking up,
Now warming; the trees taking growth again;
Groundhogs munching the greenery; clouds appearing
And vanishing by their laws; bluejay's rasp, to
Spring peepers peeping; a kid just born
In a shivering stance beside its mother;
We see the same world over and over,
Precise motions of the seasons none can stop,
The idea comes that it is as new
As fresh and real as when we saw it young,
Or younger, sense of earth as paradise.

Yet we have changed, our bodies wearing down.
No will of ours can change the laws of nature.
Speak, for we will be banished from paradise,
Love, while the flesh has the care to love,
Accept time, a whiteness now and to come
When the life of man will be
Part of the mystery of eternity.

Malevolently circling, a huge black bird
Wheels out of the sky. His eye is baleful,
Like fires of hell, he has come to kill
Your dream of paradise, and to tell
You and mankind to get off the earth,
For his black shape, his menace and his swoop
Are the annunciation of reality
As he comes toward you with authority.
You are not only driven out of paradise,
He will force you into dark beyond your will,
He will cast his shape upon you like a pall.

No bird of paradise this bird of doom.
Time makes this vulture mean. He comes
With inevitable circling silent wings,
He will not sleep, and he will blot you.

It was better to have been thrown
Out of paradise, more human to accept
Knowledge of good and evil: Eve the brightest
Of the bright, that now in darkness we must go,
Endlessly seeking the speech of truth,
Lips to find it, kiss of the word.

Adam and Eve expelled
Were better than Adam and Eve innocent.
Let a radiant wish be known
Although the black bird feast on man.

# Gene Frumkin

(June 1975)

# A VIEW OF THE ORGAN MOUNTAINS
# NORTH OF LAS CRUCES, NEW MEXICO

*for Keith and Heloise Wilson*

As a Jew in New Mexico
I'm simply another white man
who arrived too late. But in Rumania,
in the photographs Keith brought back,
I saw myself much older,
wearing a black hat and praying shawl.
I was the one honored
to carry the Torah.
                    It must have been
*mahrev,* the evening service.
There must have been at least ten of us,
otherwise I would have been elsewhere,
alone in prayer. Ten Jewish men,
still there, in one synagogue
in Rumania!
                    But I was in Las Cruces,
The Crosses, and I was there
to read poetry, not the evening scripture.
When I read, my words felt
like small flames on my lips.
How long since I'd remembered
the Land of the Fathers?

Years, many years, and not Rumania,
not even mother's Latvia or father's Lithuania.
Nor Judea itself. The Land of the Fathers
is the soil that remembers me:
in New Mexico, or anywhere on Earth.
My feet, the rhythm of my feet,
will never shake *that* dust.

# Rita Garitano

(May 1976)

# A ROOM OF HER OWN

Plath said, "Perfection is terrible,
it cannot have children."

How often I think that line,
even mutter it to myself,

folding stained clothes
that scream scrub me
as I shove them in the dresser

but there is no time for perfection
while ice cream melts in the grocery bag

and the dog that needs bathing
claws at the door.

I race through the kitchen
on legs that itch with new stubble
greasy hair flapping about my face,

bash a shin on the dishwasher door
hanging in my path like a guillotine.

Sylvia, who cleaned your kitchen
the following day?
Who ran when the children called you?

How could you take the time
to decide
that's what you wanted to do?

Were you so efficient
you made a space for yourself

but the paper you placed like a mirror
before you
was numb and dumb and blank

and the high pitched wail
of the terror of freedom
rushed through your veins.

# Dan Gerber
### (December 1971)

# A FINE EXCESS

It doesn't matter
that I've wasted thirty years
indulged myself with mindless toys
sweated problems that didn't matter
wanting to write a poem about lilacs
a poem that made some difference

I've dreamed of Walt Whitman
I've wanted to grow broader
in the chest and shoulders
wanted a dignity to replace my grin
    my all American boy

I've wanted to get free of my possessions
to be generous about America
I'd like to talk with working men
and avoid violent terms
with politicians avoiding nausea
with 'concerned citizens'
and keep from yawning
to talk with Whitman
of the origin of poems

I've spent whole evenings with my reflection
the lamp on the desk
I never learn from experience
I watch myself in the dark
the window only a plane of glass

I've read of whales that sleep in the sea
of their slaughter
heard recordings of their singing
their vain attempts to find a mate
I know of wolves and their true nature
the care of their young
their mythical dangers to man

By my fire
I read of the infinite stars
their impossible distances
the remote chance of other life
similar to our own

I'm rocked by the rise and fall of the tide
indulge in the struggle of the sea turtle
the phases of the moon seen from my window
I've scouted the coast of China
the mountains of Peru
pondered the inscrutable American mind
the subtle changes of light in November
the first crystals of ice

This morning I remembered my insane lust for travel
my mania for the telephone
my need to be left alone
all I imagine is me
I begin to regret the sound of my name
drift away with Debussy and Mahler
live through the letters of Keats
the death of Rilke
those shabby and incredible lives

# Miguel González-Gerth
(August, 1976)

# TRAGICOMIC CONCEIT

Most artists are known to turn the other cheek
And render themselves, being boldest when meek.
In words as in paint (if the subject's to write)
The strokes must show balance of shadow and light.
To paint one's own portrait is to kill and give life.
One must carefully use the fine brush, the dull knife.
Behold here a man at once rapt and afraid:
Though he is the betrayer, he looks the betrayed.

# Larry Goodell

(June 1975)

# THE POET'S APPEAL

out of
the 60's     as if their little trips could match
the age old bardic dawn
the barrelling of voices out of the ground
and into the Air, the clacking of wings & sings
around the lamp I turned on as Old Man in the Book
& come as Old Man again neither acting neither playing
saying you pay me for a little song or
I'll give it to you anyway    You Sterling Mophead
Transfixed Broom   upside down    ancestor hair
zigzag robe  & singing voices not choruses  not ah-ah-ah
um-m-m        not
indulging Priests      feeling out the gloom
not the higher prophet    in the other room
    but You
Baby    Old Mophead inverted Broom Scarecrow man
Feathered Shirt Incan
Incantational.
   Can  take
Strength in the oil of the cartilege in my bones
Lubricant  the Levers of our arms especially
to raise them in Endurance of the Dance
Stodgy stagey Women Take off your robes & reveal
Bird Costumes   Come at me as you will I am
Neither Old Man   Nor Young now   but teetering totter
the Mannikin's Daughter    Daughter's Unlimited
I thrust myself out at you & ask you for Wisdom
in this Giant Deed     Strength MopHead Father
Endurance Sisters Otter    Ought to got to ought to got to
Got Damn Rung   God Nation In betwixt
Without the English   there aint no Ointment
Our Language divides us unites us in vain
if we arent equal competitors in it
competitors in song    each doing wrong
unless he sings his song    & she takes up the adverb
& scatters out the long    rainbow

tipping head across the sky until each of us die
& down with the rainbow head   on the other side
rich as side splitters
                    the Clowns
arrive.


                        CLOWN SONG

                        O!
                        O!
                        O!
                        We gonna have
        so much fun.

# Thom Gunn
(October 1972)

# AUTOBIOGRAPHY

The sniff of the real, that's
what I'd want to get
                    how it felt
to sit on Parliament
Hill on a May evening
studying for exams      skinny
seventeen     dissatisfied
            yet sniffing such
a potent air, smell of
grass in heat from
the day's sun

I'd been walking through the damp
rich ways by the ponds
and now lay on the upper
grass with Lamartine's poems

life seemed all
loss, and what was more
I'd lost whatever it was
before I'd even had it

a green dry prospect
distant babble of children
and beyond, distinct at
the end of the glow
St Paul's like a stone thimble

longing so hard to make
inclusions that the longing
has become      in memory
an inclusion

# Drummond Hadley

(February 1971)

# SPRINGTIME

*for Diana*

Old plum tree blossom, one time I knew,
   when there was just you and I
in some long ago blooming, that over the years
   I'd forgotten in the leaf shadows of you.

When I walk up to the ridge from the tractor and the wheat field,
   over the dry ribs of arroyo sand,
    metate stone grinding in the evening sunlight by the trail,
the South wind blows me the scent of some memory,
   some old song beneath the blossoms I remember I once knew—

White arms in the sand by the roots of the tree
   as though the finger petals of those white flowers
   held the light mecate reins to my memory—

Red in the husks of the new buds pushing
   light green up the fiber of the coming stems
knowing some shadow in the old limbs
   that I'd forgotten was you—

White plum blossoms
   come down, come down,
while the buds with your dress like white flowers fall
   the folds with the clearness in your petals darken—

While the whiteness withers away
   to be gone before daylight
drops there on the sandy earth
   for our eyes to see—

      White plum tree blossom
        hurry down, come down away—

What will happen to you and me
   when we've grown old and thrown our seed
and we lie here in the sand
   near some old blossoms under a tree—

Ah plum tree blossoms
one time I knew—

While the sun and rains come and go
these springtimes pass away.
Come bloom here this springtime
in the soft light sand with me.


Metate—Indian Seed grinding stone.
Mecate—Braided, woven, or twisted rope
made from the manes or tails of horses
and used for reins in breaking colts.

# Donald Hall
(October 1972)

# KICKING THE LEAVES

## 1

Kicking the leaves, October, as we walk home together
from the game, in Ann Arbor,
on a day the color of soot, rain in the air;
I kick at the leaves of maples,
reds of seventy different shades, yellow
like old paper; and poplar leaves, fragile and pale;
and elm leaves, flags of a doomed race.
I kick at the leaves,  making a sound I remember
as the leaves swirl upward from my boot,
and flutter; and I remember
Octobers walking to school in Connecticut,
wearing corduroy knickers that swished
with a sound like leaves; and a Sunday buying
a cup of cider at a roadside stand
on a dirt road in New Hampshire; and kicking the leaves,
autumn 1955 in Massachusetts, knowing
my father would die when the leaves were gone.

## 2

Each fall in New Hampshire, on the farm
where my mother grew up, a girl in the country,
my grandfather and grandmother
finished the autumn work, taking the last vegetables in
from the cold fields, canning, storing roots and apples
in the cellar under the kitchen.  Then my grandfather
raked leaves against the house
as the final chore of autumn.
One November I drove up from college to see them.
We pulled big rakes, as we did when we hayed in summer,
pulling leaves against the granite foundation
around the house, on every side of the house,
and then, to keep them in place, we cut pine boughs
and laid them across the leaves
green on red, until the house
was tucked up, ready for snow
that would freeze the leaves in tight, like a stiff skirt.
Then we puffed through the shed door,

taking off boots and overcoats, slapping our hands,
and sat in the kitchen, rocking, and drank
black coffee my grandmother made,
three of us sitting together, silent, in gray November.


3

One Saturday when I was little, before the war,
my father came home at noon, from his half day at the office,
and wore his Bates sweater, black on red,
with the crossed hockey sticks on it, and raked beside me
in the back yard, and tumbled in the leaves with me,
laughing, and carried me, laughing, my hair full of leaves,
to the kitchen window
where my mother could see us, and smile, and motion
to set me down, afraid I would fall and be hurt.


4

Kicking the leaves today, as we walk home together
from the game, among crowds of people
with their bright pennants, as many and bright as leaves,
my daughter's hair is the red-yellow color
of birch leaves, and she is tall like a birch,
growing up, fifteen, growing older; and my son
flamboyant as maple, twenty,
visits from college, and walks ahead of us, his step
springing, impatient to travel
the woods of the earth. Now I watch them
from a pile of leaves beside this clapboard house
in Ann Arbor, across from the school
where they learned to read,
as their shapes grow small with distance, waving,
and I know that I
diminish them, not them, as I go first
into the leaves, taking
the step they will follow, Octobers and years from now.

## 5

This year the poems came back, when the leaves fell.
Kicking the leaves, I heard the leaves tell stories,
remembering, and therefore looking ahead, and building
the house of dying. I looked up into the maples
and found them, the vowels of bright desire.
I thought they had gone forever
while the bird sang I love you, I love you,
and shook its black head
from side to side, and its red eye with no lid,
through years of winter, cold
as the taste of chicken wire, the music of cinder block.

## 6

Kicking the leaves, I uncover the lids of graves.
My grandfather died at seventy-seven, in March
when the sap was running, and waits in a northern grave
where elms still drop their leaves;
and I think of my father again, dead twenty years,
coughing himself to death, at fifty-two, in the house
in the suburbs. Oh, how we flung
leaves in the air! How they tumbled and fluttered around us,
like slowly cascading water, when we walked together
in Hamden, before the war, when Johnson's Pond
had not surrendered to houses, the two of us
hand in hand, and in the wet air the smell of leaves
burning;
and in six years I will be fifty-two.

Now I fall, now I leap and fall
to feel the leaves crush under my body, to feel my body
buoyant in the ocean of leaves, rocking like the ocean.
Oh, this delicious falling into the arms of leaves,
into the soft laps of leaves!
Face down, I swim into the leaves, feathery,
breathing the acrid odor of maple, swooping
in long glides to the bottom of October,

where the farm lies curled against winter, and soup steams
its breath of onion and carrot
onto damp curtains and windows; and past the windows
the tall bare maple trunks and branches, the oak
with its few brown weathery remnant leaves,
and the pine trees, holding their green.
Now I leap and fall, exultant, recovering
from death, on account of death, in accord with the dead,
the smell and taste of leaves again,
and the pleasure, the only long pleasure, of taking a place
in the story of leaves.

# Joy Harjo
(June 1975)

# THE LAST SONG

how can you stand it
he said
the hot oklahoma summers
where you were born
this humid thick air
is choking me
and i want to go back
to new mexico

it is the only way
i know how to breathe
an ancient chant
that my mother knew
came out of a history
woven from wet tall grass
in her womb
and i know no other way
than to surround my voice
with the summer songs of crickets
in this moist south night air

oklahoma will be the last song
i'll ever sing

# Michael S. Harper

(April 1973)

# GRANDFATHER

In 1915 my grandfather's
neighbors surrounded his house
near the dayline he ran
on the Hudson
in Catskill, NY
and thought they'd burn
his family out
in a movie they'd just seen
and be rid of his kind:
the death of a lone black
family is *the Birth
of a Nation*,
or so they thought.
His 5'4'' waiter gait
quenched the white jacket smile
he'd brought back from watered
polish of my father
on the turning seats,
and he asked his neighbors
up on his thatched porch
for the first blossom of fire
that would burn him down.

They went away, his nation,
spittooning their torched necks
in the shadows of the riverboat
they'd seen, posse decomposing;
and I see him on Sutter
with white bag from your
restaurant, challenged by his first
grandson to a foot-race
he will win in white clothes.

I see him as he buys galoshes
for his railed yard near Mineo's
metal shop, where roses jump
as the el circles his house
toward Brooklyn, where his rain fell;
and I see cigar smoke in his eyes,-
chocolate Madison Square Garden chews

he breaks on his set teeth,
stitched up after cancer,
the great white nation immovable
as his weight wilts
and he is on a porch
that won't hold my arms,
or the legs of the race run
forwards, or the film
played backwards on his grandson's eyes.

# Jim Harrison

(November 1970)

## JIM—AGE 38, 5'10'', W.196,
## STRAPPING GOGGLE-EYED NORDIC BANKRUPT

I widowed my small
collection of magic
until it poisoned itself with longing.
I have learned nothing.
I give orders to the rain.
I tried to catch the tempest in a gill net.
The stars seem a little closer lately.
I'm no longer afraid to die
but is this a guidepost of lunacy?
I intend to see the 10 hundred million worlds Manjusri
passed through before he failed to awaken the maiden.
Taking off and landing are the dangerous times.
I was commanded in a dream to dance.

# George Hitchcock

## (December 1969)

# FUGUE AND VARIATIONS

So it's you?
Yes it's me.
I thought so.
You did?
Yes I did.
Did what?
Thought so.

Heliotrope.    Patchouli.
Delineations of wet nooses
The door risen from the dead, the throat
which has choked on lace.

It's a matter of fabricating the seething feet.
It's a question of the gold-rimmed warts.
Of authenticating the least follicles.

This lamp has been—
Reserved?
Yes, reserved.
Now?
Or presently.
By whom?
Does it matter?
By whose order?
Does it matter?

Does it matter?

Dusk comes over the horizon like a cowboy.
In the vestibules of soap darkness is king.
The Choctaw nations are tipped into the sea
while each April another government
evaporates at the Finland station.

You shrugged?
Unavoidably.
Noncommittally?
Unavoidably.  The fact is—

The fact is there are terrorists in the player piano.
They have exploded our dentures.
They openly boast of chromatic fantasies.

Chopin appears in the mahogany frame.
Berlioz inaugurates the Stadt-Theater;
he is giddy from the long sea voyage.
The curtain has opened on the insect comedy:
the flies, saturated in musk,
sing in tender silver voices heavy with torn vodka:
*Voi sapete, quel che fa.*

Now everything bursts into light—
the scabbard the spool the swollen flag
the stone guest on the phosphorescent stair.
It is not the destruction of the dream but the dream itself.
It is not the epoch of Saturn but the slaughter of smoke.
The key turns twenty times.
The walls will not open.
The walls will never open.

I hold out my hand to incoherence.

# Ann Marie (Haralambie) Huck

(May 1976)

# INTO YOUR HANDS

the cloistered afternoons
spring full-cassocked
from my mother mornings

the glass in the window deepens
barely penetrable blue
candle smoke incense smoke
rising together to wrap me robed
chalice and ciborium in the cupboard

but morning always shatters
midnight's scapular and Office
alone in my cloister
for just this while at least
mother agonistes
mother priest
mother agony

the morning is the joy
of fist held weeds
pitchers of lemonade
mother omnipotent

oh my child
I am a child myself
*bless me father*
*for I have sinned*
*forgive them Father*

the child of the child
children of the Father
where do we go
turn to the May altar
mother to Mother

suffer the cross
*suffer the little children*
how do we come

together we enter the cloister
brown robed bowed
genuflect before the tabernacle

yet out you run
to brightness to open playgrounds
flight from the camel's eye
as if it were here
as if I could find it

maybe if I follow you
*suffer the little children to come*

I watch
knees pounding prie Dieu
fist beating breast
*bless me father*

May the Lord accept the sacrifice
*de manibus tuis*
*manibus meis*

annoint me
the chrism opening my soul
opening Your house

*I believe*
*Lord help my unbelief*

# James Humphrey
(March 1972)

# TO THE YOUNG POETS, EXCEPT CHILDREN,
## WHO HAVEN'T EARNED THE TITLE
## BUT CALL THEMSELVES POETS ANYWAY

You aren't a sun
diving sea-wide. She's

not the sea, poised
or scaled, taking

your blood, leaving
your arm-pits green.

The sea is there, yes.
The sky is there. Both

are there, indifferent
to you.

There is the apprenticeship
to deal with. There is no

magic wand. Be direct
with your feelings

and thoughts. Go from there.
But quit trying to con me

and poetry. Poetry is fighting
for its breath

# David Ignatow

(February 1971)

# THE EXPLORER

I have this mountain to climb
and no one to stop me,
this dangerous mountain
of glaciers and gaunt cliffs,
and I will climb it for the sake
of the living.  Climb, then,
they call out, and die.
Climb, then, I answer softly,
and live.
I am about to begin.

I am reaching for possession.
Climb, then, they whisper, and live.
Climb, then, I reply strongly, and die.

My joy is in the trees and grass,
the rocks and glacial face of the mountain.
My joy is skyward, my life is the opening
of heaven. I have placed my foot
on the mountain that I have discovered
is my brain.  I am the joyful man.

# Lawson Fusao Inada

(January 1972)

# CAPTION, CIRCA 1972

Look at me.
If I came up to you
about that time,
I'd probably
be smiling.

I mean the family
was healthy;
I was young,
feeling young,
with places to go.

I dried my socks
in the Tucson
winter sun.

I could take a song
like ''Asian-America''
and use it,
strong at the mouth,
a place to stay,
and know.

Like Nogales,
breaking down over
Veracruzana
and never be south
but home,

the West Fresno
jukebox always going . . .

America was smoldering
Asians wherever
it says it goes.

I met the great
granddaughter
of Sadakichi Hartmann
cool and sweet
in Phoenix.

He roamed the heat
of the Morongo
Reservation, crazy
with poetry,
the music of images . . .

History has a weak
way of running
over at the mouth,
the insanity of images . . .

Once again, I'm the lone
Jap on these pages.

Look at me.
You goddamn rights
I can be happy.

# Jeremy Ingalls

(October 1964)

## TRAITS: INNER PORTRAIT

New England's mytilus, its old-blue tidal shell,
And Arizona's turquoise will in time's spin shatter
Along with every bone-plate once a human skull.

The sometimes satiric, never sardonic, mildly ironic smile
Reflects the major commedia, the Galilean's own
Charge: never to ostracize nor throw a stone nor pick a bone
Nor ever sophisticate the also real
Anguish of humanness as though no matter,
The earth's volcanic callousness and the willfully cruel
Penchant in humankind to flaunt a less than kindly will.

The soul, suppose, endures, hers, his, and yours.
Each one, reputed to weigh nothing, then weighs in,
Both firm and pliant, weighing, and last weighable.
Another scale at last may weigh what may
Beyond time's scale be durable.

# Will Inman

(May 1976)

# LATE ADVISORY FOR INTERGALACTIC TRAVELLERS
## SUCH AS POETS

stars, larger than sun, are pores vibrating
in God's terrible black tongue o those sounds
would scorch my ears dared i listen.  no.
silence in my hearing is safer far
than one syllable from such implacable
thirst.

       Did you hear That Voice?
you're sure?  no.  you were but self-deceived.
no one could hear that and survive.  Relax.
we shall not be so easily shed of you.
count silences for extra years,
heal your terror with joyous weeping;
i tell you, you did not hear That Sound.

o between laps of thunder you have dug up
a tongueless bell.
let its cup tremble distantly
with those galactic hungerings.

even then, those vibrations can
digest you down to the infinite gut
unless you know when   and dare
to sing your own song.

# June Jordan
(November 1971)

# UNTITLED

These poems
they are things that I do
in the dark
reaching for you
whoever you are
and
are you ready?

These words
they are stones in the water
running away

These skeletal lines
they are desperate arms for my longing and love.

I am a stranger
learning to worship the strangers
around me

whoever you are
whoever I may become.

# Donald Justice
(April 1970)

# SELF-PORTRAIT AS STILL LIFE

The melon on the table,
Plump, unspoiled.
Close by, the knife,
Patient lover.

It smiles. It knows
How attractive it is
To sunlight. It can wait.
The guitar on the wall,

Succumbing to shadow,
To drowsiness, to dream,
Remembering hands,
Beginning to dance now

Somewhere inside,
There, there where the heart's
Most resonant, most empty . . .
And where am I? I don't

Come into the picture.
Poets, O fellow exiles,
Lisping your pure Spanish,
It's your scene now, and welcome.

You take up the guitar.
You cut up the melon.
Myself, I'm not about to
Disturb the composition.

# Rolly Kent
(May 1976)

# AFTER THE STORMY NIGHT

In the morning, dark moons
sailed in the orange tree.
I was zipping my pants when I saw them,
through the window.

"Look what the storm has done," I thought,
and went out in my socks to be near them
while the sun dried my hair.

Cold globes of sleep,
one for each hand.
Holding hands with a tree.

Maybe I just closed my eyes.

Or stared into the hedge. The dirt.
The roof-tiles along the hill.

A pigeon circled.  Dust stood still in the light.
I could see the air.

One by one the morning took its turns:

a man, bare-chested on the corner,
looking straight up; two spiders
descending the woodpile; some frost in shadow
like a heart-shaped field of snow—
one by one, proceeding.

You called me from the kitchen then,
said my name like Fido and whistled twice.

And maybe my eyes were closed. There was no man
when I looked,
no bird, spiders, heart,
no hard, dark moons.

I took my hands into the kitchen
and warmed them on your eyes.
"Oooo," you said, "guess who."

We sat at the table quietly,
eating your strange cakes and butter.

# Karl Kopp

(June 1975)

# THE HANGING MAN

Shoveling dung in Denver's field
I stop from time to time    look up
lean on my shovel
the sky in motion
fast low clouds from the Gulf
those trees . . .

    till one cow blunders close
horned like a bull
Look I don't want trouble
Git
      when from the barn a sudden cry
(I'd thought it empty
but a calf of course
not two weeks old so Denver told me)
this its mother with bulk and horn
to brave the man-thing
(and now I see she trembles)

It's okay
I have my own young son to guard
to love so hard it sometimes shakes me too
depending for a season
with legs arms back and brain
   and then as I approach to touch her
see the rain-soaked streets again
the noisy stalls young soldiers
still in battle gear
among the jostling tourists    beckoned
by multilingual guides
to Calvary the Tomb the Wailing Wall
the war before last  the calf
crouched by its mother's side
hung on a hook for sale    shuddering
whimpering knock-kneed life roped
to a quartered carcass
as the soldiers pass   rifles in sling
muzzles down

but all arrive attached above
until cut loose we die   so much
seasoning for trees and grass
unless we see to richer harvests.

   she leaves me
somehow trusting  returns
to graze on vetch and rye

the sky hangs on the haft of my shovel
I see black loam beneath my boots
my work half-done

# Maxine Kumin

(January 1975)

# BODY AND SOUL: A MEDITATION

Mornings, after leg lifts and knee bends,
I go up in a shoulder stand.
It's a form of redress. My
winter melancholy hangs
upside down. All my organs
reverse their magnetic fields:
ovaries bob on their eyestalks,
liver, kidneys, spleen, whatever
is in there functioning unseen
free-float like parachutes,
or so it seems from plough position,
legs behind my head, two
big toenails grazing the floor.

Body, Old Paint, Old Partner,
I ought to have paid closer
attention when Miss Bloomberg
shepherded the entire fifth grade
into the Walk-Through Woman.
I remember going
up three steps, all right,
to enter the left auricle.
I remember the violet light
which made it churchly
and the heartbeat amplified
to echo from chamber to chamber
like God speaking unto Moses.

But there was nothing about the soul,
that miner's canary flitting
around the open spaces;
no diagram in which
the little ball-bearing soul
bumbled her way downhill
in the pinball machine
of the interior, clicking
against the sternum,
the rib cage, the pelvis.
The Walk-Through Woman ceased
shortly below the waist.
Her genitals were off limits.

Perhaps there the soul
had set up housekeeping?
Perhaps a pullman kitchen,
a one-room studio
in an erogenous zone?
O easy erogenous zones!
Flashing lights, detour
and danger signs in
the sprouting pubic hair
. . . tilt!
Alas, I emerged from
the right ventricle
little the wiser.

Still unlocated, drifting,
my airmail half-ounce soul
shows up from time to time
like those old-fashioned
doctors who used to cheer
their patients in girls' boarding schools
with midnight bedside visits.
Body, Old Paint, Old Partner
in this sedate roundup we ride,
going up the Mountain in
the meander of our middle age
after the same old cracked tablets,
though soul and we touch tongue,

somehow it seems less sure;
somehow it seems we've come
too far to get us there.

# Philip Levine

(April 1972)

# BREATH

Who hears the humming
of rocks at great height,
the long steady drone
of granite holding together,
the strumming of obsidian
to itself? I go among
the stones stooping
and pecking like a
sparrow, imagining
the glacier's final push
resounding still. In
a freezing mountain
stream, my hand opens
scratched and raw and
flutters strangely,
more like an animal
or wild blossom in wind
than any part of me. Great
fields of stone
stretching away under
a slate sky, their single
flower the flower
of my right hand.
                        Last night
the fire died into itself
black stick by stick
and the dark came out
of my eyes flooding
everything. I
slept alone and dreamed
of you in an old house
back home among
your country people,
among the dead, not
any living one besides
yourself. I woke
scared by the gasping
of a wild one, scared
by my own breath, and
slowly calmed

remembering your weight
beside me all these
years, and here and
there an eye of stone
gleamed with the warm light
of an absent star.
                    Today
in this high clear room
of the world, I squat
to the life of rocks
jewelled in the stream
or whispering
like shards. What fears
are still held locked
in the veins till the last
fire, and who will calm
us then under a gold sky
that will be all of earth.
Two miles below on the burning
summer plains, you go
about your life one
more day. I give you
almond blossoms
for your hair, your hair
that will be white, I give
the world my worn-out breath
on an old tune, I give
it all I have
and take it back again.

# John Logan

(May 1976)

# THE SEARCH

But for whom do I look?
The whole long night you will see me walk
or maybe during the day
watch me pass by.
But I do not wander—
It is a search. For I stop here,
or here, wherever people gather.
Depot, restaurant, bar.
But whom do I seek?
You will see me coming back
perhaps at dawn. Sometimes
the faces seem like tombs.
I have tried to read the names
so long my eyes darken in their graves
of bone. (The bodies of our eyes
lie side by side
and do not touch.)
But for whom do I look? My search
is not for wife, daughter or for son
for time to time
it has taken me from them.
Or has wrenched me from my friend:
I will abruptly leave him,
and I do not go home.
For whom do I seek? Out of what fear?
It is not for queers,
for my search leads me from their bars.
It is not for whores,
since I reject their wares,
or another time may not.
Then for whom do I look?
When I was young I thought
I wanted (yearned for) older age.
Now I think I hunt with so much rage
that I will risk or lose
family or friends for the ghost of my youth.
Thus I do not know for what I look.
Father? Mother?
The father who will be the mother?
Sister who will be the brother?

Often I hunt in the families of others—
until hope scatters.
I will call up friend or student at night
or I will fly
to see them—will bask and heal in the warm
places of their homes.
And I must not be alone
no matter what needs be done,
for then my search is ended.
So now the panicked thumbs of my poem pick
through the grill. They poke
the lock
and put out a hand and then an arm.
The limbs of my poems
come within your reach.
Perhaps it is you whom I seek.

# Archibald MacLeish

(November 1965)

# HEBRIDES

Old men live in a life
as the Gaels in those ocean islands,
a croft by the sea and a wife
and sons for a while;

afterward wife and croft
and the sound of the sea and the thought of it,
children and all gone off
over the water;

even the eldest son,
even the youngest daughter,
all of them vanished and gone
by the way of the water.

A man and his wife, those two,
left on the ocean island:
they talk as the old will do
and they nod and they smile

but they think of their sons, how they laughed,
and she calls but it's not for them—
"she'd rather a kitten to have
than a child to remember."

You can live too long in a life
where the sons go off and the daughter
off over sea and the wife
watches the water.

## Carolyn Maisel

(June 1975)

# from PIG WOMAN

She wants to seduce a homosexual Jesuit.
Her womb is a red monastery, her heart
bleeds in it. Her desire is a prayer. She
repents her old sins. New ones come to her
like cousins to a rich funeral. Her friend
says, well, why didn't you scream at him,
"you queer, you can't even recognize a good
piece when you see one." Pig woman is not
sure what he has recognized. Mortality
is a killing joy. A force-field of events
built up popping energy, somewhere a blindness
sets in. She is robed like the Virgin
attended by Compassion and Death. Pierced
parts of anatomy in a gold cup. She
has eaten up her salvation. Little one eye,
two eyes, three eyes, it's better
not to see too much. Her friends
come out of the closet. Their thirsty
passions spent in some arid garden of family,
they announce themselves like intimate strangers.
One eye blinded for sex, two for freedom, and the
third for pure suffering. These are the new saints.
She prays for everyone, mostly herself.

# Howard McCord

(June 1975)

# JENNIFER

You are the woman
who makes things clear.

The excitement of clarity
is more profound
than the burning of a star,
or the necessary slip
of coin to the Algonquin's
bellhops.

I see you there, in a tall
chair along the west paneled wall,
reading, sipping a drink,
waiting with the poise
of a flower designed by Brahms.

(I am listening to Symphony #4)

and everything is clear.

It has never been necessary
for us to ask.

*Clarity*.

We hone it subtly
as a creature dances
who has no name.

# Sandra McPherson
(March 1973)

# 1943

I was born the year of the gray pennies.
They'll find me in another layer, the skull
Above the deviating Lincoln heads

Worth ten or fifteen cents by now.
The smile won't be in the bone,
So they will think that I've depreciated.

But that money didn't last. Gray did
And camouflaged our war,
Woodchucks, catbirds—

The year of our birth sank beneath us.
The bank was rock.
On top of me are falling all the saved.

# William Meredith
## (March 1970)

# WHERE I'M STAYING NOW

(In April, 1971, before I had any thought of the characteriza-
tion of Hazard, the Painter, I wrote this little self-portrait as it
appears below. Later that year, when I had written four of the
sections of *Hazard*, I conveyed it to him as part of the series of
16 poems that were finished in 1974. Resemblances between
the life and character of Hazard, I wrote in a prefatory note,
and those of the author are not disclaimed but are much fewer
than the author would like.)

1.  I look out of these two holes, or I run
    to the other two and listen. Am I trapped in here?

2.  I have had on this funny suit for years, it's getting
    baggy, but I can still move all the parts.

3.  In the top I can make satisfying noises.
    I fill it again & again with things I want.
    It does not like them all. I empty it furtively.

4.  It is rubbery and durable. I wash it.
    People sometimes touch it, that feels good
    although I am deep inside.

5.  I do not find it absurd. Is this because
    I am used to it? (trapped in it? Where are we?
    This is certainly not rubber or a cheap plastic.)

6.  If I crawl out of it at night, it comes
    snuffling after me & swallows me—
    it says it is looking for words.
    I tell it it has come to the wrong man.

# Carol Merrill

(June 1975)

# PORTRAIT

Mom really knows how to pick 'em.
First one beat her up twice—my dad.
He flies airplanes and I'm not supposed to see him,
But I call him with the stash of dimes
He left me when he left.
I would like to learn how to fly,
But mom says I won't ever.
We're moving to Weatherford, Oklahoma,
For her to study pharmacy.
Another little town. I don't have a home
And my grandmother feels bad about that,
So she's going to will me her farm someday.
I get to know people best on the bus
between new towns.
She's leaving the second one now
who also beat her up.
A rodeo cowboy—his face smashed bad
So you pat his cheek, and it looks OK
But you press and there's nothing there
You just push through his face.
A bull got him because he wore a white hat
instead of his black one; coincidence
I said, but he said he knows better.
A wicked woman gave him the white hat.
He left the hospital too soon
Took all the pins out of his face
And the bones just dissolved on one side.
My uncle and cousin fought him one night late,
Chased each other and crashed in my bedroom door.
Beat each other with the door
Until it was in little pieces.
Woke me up.  He promised me a pony
But gave away two to my brothers.
I never got to keep one,
So I guess I don't care
If we leave the second one.
He wasn't my real daddy anyway.
And I wouldn't let anybody say so.

(To Becky Fulton. I hope you learn to fly, honey.)

# Christopher Middleton

(August 1976)

# SNAKE ROCK

Tall snake without strut or buttress
snake which talks in the rhythm of chemicals
snake with legs

tell me where the spyholes are
come between my sheets and just be yourself
snake with two breasts which look at me

snake with hair and very tender armpits
show me the moon
show me the moon or must I split your skull
tell me

tell me animal with fruits
animal of cellulose and lignin come into my house
animal with leaves
cambium animal come into my house

animal which sucks minerals out of the dirt
tell me animal drinking the sun
dead centered animal shaping sugar into wood

drinking lakes also towering flower
tell me how you can change the sun into yourself
flower with a snout
rock with claws come into my kitchen
tell me how you can cook the air and crunch its bones

flower with fur
flower with padded feet smelling of incense
snake who stands in the suchness of silence
come to my table of wood and wickerwork

flower with white teeth
calcium flower teach me the revolution
rock with jaws which bite the flies and all flesh
tell me tell me the rain

snake with a wet nose tell me the lightning
tree which snorts and twitches
umbel snoozing with bristles of soft wire

flower which runs across the street suddenly
tell me how you die
tell me how you die without having to think of it

# John Newlove

(March 1965)

# OF MY OWN FLESH

Hard crystals there are hard crystals inside them
in their bellies and their hands
curl up when they talk to you their eyes narrow
as if the sun were burning into them
and they smile

They smile their lips
draw back stiffly from the pale enamelled teeth the pain
cramping the cheek muscles is shown
in the grooves cut in their faces in
the eyebrows

They wish they would turn to stone they hate
to have feeling they hate you
for feeling it is not right they think
for me to be careful not to hurt
because I want to hurt

In the ball of my clenched hand talons are growing
it is the palm of my own flesh they enter
they ought to be furrowing yours
it is your skin that should be ripped
your blood flowing

Hard crystals I have hard crystals in my belly
claws are growing where my nails were
my heels are round stones to grind you
my muscles bunch to kill you
to cut you to see blood

I am becoming a statue
here in the glare of my own dead eyes
I am becoming a statue

The Fieries and the Snuffies

John Frederick Nims

(April 1964)

# OUR HERO

Having produced lizards eighty feet long,
Claws curved like anchors, skull a hungry bowl;
Cockroaches, scales vibrant as a gong—
The country he was born in turned to coal.

His brother was a poodle-faced baboon.
His sister—shhh—we don't mention her;
Her work was steady. Heads shrunk like a prune,
Hooks, faggots, ropes show what his kinfolk were.

But fortunately, when all's said and done,
He inherited from his father a small infinity;
Invested it (it seemed twice he was gone)
Whence came some true and much absurd divinity,

Some tunes, a little rime or two, some ochre
On caves and cloth, books saying what books meant.
Always he drew the face-card or the joker.
Dreamed of a Golden Age—this malcontent.

# Susan North

(May 1976)

# RUMOR YOU CALLED MY NAME

the other one
that no one knows
so here is everything with answers
and nothing without defense
while inside my muffled garment of fear
what I need to say
leans up against itself
and mumbles

if I had the comfort
of coincidence I'd wear it
but there are no accidents
and I am falling between long bricked buildings
between windows blinking like buttons
falling faster than soot straighter than stone
falling like knowing like dread
and survival is no longer enough
my arms shedding their skins
the skins peeling their scars
my hand tearing its webs
my mouth in its prayer
*any day now it will be*
*my turn*

# Steve Orlen

(February 1976)

# NO QUARTER

*Steve Ferreira   1949-1976*

Limping among hookers and drunks, he says he's done it all,
As hunter and hunted, his wide mouth open. Tonight
He seems boyish, his head strangely large for his body.
He's brooding because his father left the sea for a woman,
Bad luck for a Portuguese. Now one brother's in jail
And the other sits banging his head against walls.
The bars along the side streets are closing. After hours,
The silences between the squares of the city keep us
At arm's length, a kind of grace, and the passing girls
Refuse his glance. Here is his motto, he says, what he means
Beyond the details of a life: "No love, no loss."

He pauses at the alley's mouth, leans into my listening
Face and says he's meaner than any man, and points
A finger for proof. The chipped teeth and caved-in brow
Are the bad debts of a thief who preys on thieves.
He searches among the tangled veins in the scarred
Crook of his arm for the path from heart to brain,
The softest sac, where there is no love and no loss,
No temptation to exist beyond this resting place. He fixes me
With his small, blurred eyes to say he's never killed
Except by accident, scared that he will, then squeezes me
To show how gentle he is, my pal, my shadow more loving than any man.

# Simon J. Ortiz

(May 1976)

# MORNING SMALLFIRE
# IN LUKACHUKAI MOUNTAINS

*Summer 1975*

Think of friends.
Think of children.
Prayer:  this morning
I walked over to the edge of a cliff
and stood by a water course on stone.
And prayed in a manner
I never have before, in humility
and for the ways I wish
I never lived.
         Prayed
for health, safety, courage,
good thoughts and vision
and love for my children,
my wife, everyone, everything.
And cried. And then I fed them,
saying,
         'Grandfathers, Grandmothers,
Kuupeshtaiyah, All-Spirit, I stand
before you in the midst
of this Mountain place,
a humbled man.  Please look on me
with your power, concern, and love.
Teach and allow me to know
your strength and peace
which I need badly these days.'
And thanking them, I fed them
peanuts and raisins because
I had nothing else—my father
says, 'That's alright, give
whatever you do have.'
I offered myself, truly,
saying, 'It will come, it will happen,
it will continue that way.'

Sitting here this morning
by my smallfire, I don't feel
like a fugitive at all.

# Raymond R. Patterson

(November 1971)

# PERFORMANCE

The Keeper unlocks the cage
And I come out with a bound,
Dressed in my animal rage

To dance these sad bones round,
A grin strapped to my snout.
It is my time to act

*The Play of the Dark and the Bars,*
The cue of the Keeper's kick
Lurking behind each trick,

The spotlights flashing like stars.
The music's in the fur.
The humor's in the chance

That I am dangerous
That I know what I dance
That we are who we are

That someone may forget.
But I am no one's pet.
The Keeper wears a scar.

## Bill Pearlman
(June 1975)

# NEW MEXICO SKY

What does this sky mean to you?
What world inhabited, cared for, lost
and magnified with memory?
Things born of bodies joined
hand in hand over a trail—
I am lightly looking everywhere
behind, within, what (again)
is this bright glory of firmament
ever so shining in my need
to grow a likeness to beauty
here where I sit below
grateful to have come so far

# Charles Potts
(June 1975)

# MARCH WARDROBE

i carry my poems
in a canvas sack
i found my socks
at the laundermat
pants i traded
with a black ex-con
its his belt
holds them up

a hand knit scarf
wrapped on my neck
the watch i keep
was a christmas gift
a dead mans gloves
now warm my hands
they are not mates

# Leroy Quintana

(May 1976)

# UNTITLED

Grandfather never went to school
spoke only a few words of English

a quiet man; when he talked
talked about simple things
planting corn or about the weather
sometimes about herding sheep as a child

One day pointed to the four directions
taught me their names
        El Norte

Poniente                                  Oriente
        El Sur

He spoke their names as if they were
one of only a handful of things
a man needed to know

Now I look back
only two generations removed
realize I am nothing but a poor fool
who went to college

trying to find my way back
to the center of the world
where Grandfather stood
that day

# A.K.Ramanujan

(February 1971)

# SELF-PORTRAIT

I resemble everyone
but myself, and sometimes see
in shop-windows,
    despite the well-known laws
    of optics,
the portrait of a stranger,
date unknown,
often signed in a corner
by my father.

## John Crowe Ransom
(March 1967)
deceased

# PIAZZA PIECE

I am a gentleman in a dustcoat trying
To make you hear. Your ears are soft and small
And listen to an old man not at all,
They want the young men's whispering and sighing.

But see the roses on your trellis dying
And hear the spectral singing of the moon;
For I must have my lovely lady soon,
I am a gentleman in a dustcoat trying.

I am a lady young in beauty waiting
Until my truelove comes, and then we kiss.
But what grey man among the vines in this
Whose words are dry and faint as in a dream?
Back from my trellis, Sir, before I scream!
I am a lady young in beauty waiting.

# George Reavey
(April 1967)
deceased

# THE FOUR WALLS OF MY CAGE

Word, smash the four walls of my cage,
The four imprisoning reasons,
The four strong empires of my age,
And all four-footed seasons.

Word, break the gravity of earth,
And tide the ghost above the air,
Defter than water in your strength,
More absolute than fire.

Word, shake the laws of history
Which herd us in, clamp down:
Unseal the white-lipped mystery
Of rood and rose and crown.

Word, ban the blind that pull me West,
The rude who draw me North,
The slaves that chain me in the East,
And lusts that hurry South.

Word, launch the rocket of my praise
For who returns no more
Where every rule divides my ways
And feelings into four.

Word, smash the four walls of my cage,
The four imprisoning reasons,
The four strong empires of my age,
And all four-footed seasons.

# Peter Redgrove

(November 1971)

## from THE BARBERS

### II.

The barber cuts the beard.
It is a mode of fathering.
We control our face-hair in Oneida county.
Never have your beard cut by a younger man.
A room of thrones and transformations.
The flies totter out pale-faced, clean-shaven;
A man sheds years in front of this gilded mirror,
You can stuff a pillow with his soft years.
It is also where the fedora gangsters
Start out from the sunny sidewalk
Pumping charred holes into the shrouded shoulders.

### IV.

The one clean-shaven like a white grape
Affronts no man; he is an egg.  The barber
Bishops this rendering monkish, Lord
Of the Numerous Transformations of Skins
And Renewal Coming of Itself.
We cut and trim to make our plots
And express ourselves in repose.
Where is that fortyniner with the ankle-length beard?
He has stepped out of it.  Is he
That youth with the 'tash?
Or that monk in the suit?

### V.

The nibbling digits, the glittering scissor-blades
Busy like feeding fish among the scalps,
The whetted razor on the supple strops,
The pungent flasks of vivid toiletries,
The flat condoms in casual packets sold
To any comer with face-hair.

## VI.

He renews his face each morning, shaving
Round his moustache, male destiny;
We do not tattoo the face to make our blazon,
It is a choice and selections of hair!
I try out beards in the bearded mirror,
Watchful as Zapata, pure as Solzhenitzyn,
His stiff upper lip shaved very naked,
Dapper as Van Dyke, pointless as Empson,
And in my own person
Laugh as an egg laughs.
I want to laugh
With teeth among the hair.


## IX.

Here is his coffin.  And here the barber comes
With his other coffin full of all the hair
He shed since his father took him for a shave.
That was like a first communion.
This is needed for the resurrection.

# Marina Rivera

(June 1976)

# EVEN

You look for her
brown even in the sternum
supporting beige ribs
that bellow tan sacks
expelling puffs
        brown, brown even in winter

you look for her
someone you could crack
down the noseline
between the breasts
and lower see
brown organs, brown blood
brown bone even

these words some want spun
are a game and those of us
who have learned the game
have triangular hearts
that spin on axis that gyrate
toward white toward brown
toward ourselves most often

so long on edges
how to rest there
by nails, by teeth
breasts to the rim
and legs draping . . .
one way: to gather
edges like dry wood
make a bed, a bridge
lie on it, watch them

our lives are mouths
no matter how the jaw placed
the teeth don't seal
they buckle here we point them
out so when you point at our lives
you get it straight.

# W.A. Roecker
(February 1971)

# 45TH PARALLEL SULKS

I'm coming down the wooded freeway
near Salem, cresting the earth
halfway between equator and pole.

Something changes at the juncture.
Oregon's ryegrass fields flame
after harvest, so much burnt chaff in the air
the mountains go up the road in disgust.

But at sundown an hour south
a rowdy wave of blackbirds shifts
over new stubble, breaking any straight
line possible, drifting like quick smoke
through cottonwoods and scrub oak.

*Home,* I think, *the next thing
we have when we're alive.*

I can feel myself cool, thin out
into a low blanket of fog
for the land.

# Orlando Romero

(May 1976)

# SELF-PORTRAIT

The little Americano children are
told they are brought by the stork.
I was told an eagle from Truchas
dropped me accidentally in the
middle of the corn field.

Little Americano children are told
to read books so as to make understanding clearer.
I was told that all that existed under the sun,
between the moon and the stars,
is not mine to understand but to contemplate.

Little Americano children are given mathematical
formulas, scientific ideology,
and are carried about by great transient machines
of metal and speed.
I was told the maize seed was planted at a depth
half of my middle finger, that the order of things
is mysterious but exemplary,
And that restlessness is contradictory to peace.

Little Americano children are given parties,
a dog for a pet and a toy shovel to play in the
Sand.
I was given penitential acceptance into a mystical-
Brotherhood at age seven,
a trained dog to work the sheep,
and a shovel that calloused my hands during irrigation,
the annual cleaning of the ditches,
and the digging of my Great-Grandfather's grave.

Little Americano children are given opportunity
I was given life.

# William Pitt Root

(December 1972)

# SONGS OF WAKING

## 1. Song of Shedding Light & Darkness

Stars
    stars
  & grass deepening
the dark fields

No one
    walks here
  with me & I feel
the hillside moving

as I move
    enclosed
  by stars, abrasive
& careless, turning

around me
    grinding
  light & the darkness
from my skin, skin

from my
    bones until
  blind & clean
I am ready to go on

## 2. Song of Presence

I let go of my darkness I have grieved there & been lost

I lay down in greenshining grasses smelling of them & rolling
   in them
I wake up in the dew where innumerable worlds orient &
   balance
  the sun recurring in each drop rounded by the light
  & Earth rounded by our star's radiance
I wake up to the water wake up light wake dew grass &
   stones
  wake eyes & ears wake the pink cloud of my bones
  & old loves & new fulfill my spirit's waking

I wake up Lord
I wake up to this blazing coat of joys
   no grief destroys

Jerome Rothenberg
(February 1971)

## from THE COUNTER-DANCES OF DARKNESS

. . . . . . .

As I dreamed my stature (mad dream!) as in the pasture at night
among the freaks, the many-headed cattle, loiterers—
that I could match their size—that bewildering bruteness,
could be set apart where I walked to be mocked—
this monster, this debaser, broken & degenerate & eternally damned
   & alone—
only not to be whole—a part of that order, the goad for its sense-
   less stars—
not to give live & watch it taken back again—
what wars in a single lifetime! what slow deaths worse than all
   wars!
what bliss as the body dissolves, turns sour, returns to its piti-
   less earth!
does a flower offend you?
does the sun make you cringe that opens every inch of you with
   careless fingers?
for this I had made myself monstrous!
how many others must die to force once moment of doubt to your
   throat?

# Ricardo Sánchez

(June 1975)

## —CASI-GATO AKA CARNEDECHIVO
## NEÉ RICARDO SÁNCHEZ (SOMETIMES!)—

a string of acronyms
course their serpentine way
after my name,
quetzales and locuras
merging
in the chiaroscuro
of reality and fantasy,
defining
barrio barriers, army,
prison, more barrios,
prisons, movement involvement,
scars of/by universities,
legions of boudoir fancies
and happenstances,
soixante-neufing fandangoes, ay,
i laugh
in my solitudes
at real and/or imagined
credientials
and doing so
uptights
an already uptighted menagerie
of academicians,
and though i laugh
when i write out my name
and its acronymed convolutions,
realization hurts
when i hurl out past/present
in the whimsy
of half jokingly saying
i am
Ricardo Sánchez, CDD, GED, BL, MD,
                        PhD, SV, CS, PPJ*,
for in the cábula
of survival
as a Chicano from barrios & prisons
exist(s)
the anomie and desolation of
numberless nights/days & even years
when light and darkness
were one and the same . . .

marked, like many another invisible person, by almost not realizing
                                                          my existence,
i travel light years into nebulous and hopeful futures,
sutured
by need
and buoyed
by hope,
life and poetry merge
into politicized primal screaming
brought on by urgency,
roads of life pocked by death and hectic loving, each caress by wind
etches
meaning on brow,
while each view of hunger in my barrios unfurls fury in mindsoul,

forced to survive
within a seemingly foreign world,
culture becomes the only weapon and shield left
with which to defend/protect
whatever cosmicity might beat
its primordiality in being-ness . . .

looking back
from being
a phd from union graduate school
to having experienced
a one to twenty five year sentence
in california (soledad) when but 19
to a twelve year sentence
in texas (huntsville & ramsey one farm)
when 25 and out by 29,
now 36 and still questing
after publishing canto y grito mi liberación
and hechizospells,
having been poet in residence via
national endowment of the arts at epcc,
still realize
that like all humanized or dehumanized beings
i carry the scars and the caresses
of my experience—i yearn and hope and strive to love
beyond the shoddy confines
of societalization,

and still the question rises out
from a heap of happenings,
culling out of memory and awareness
the awryness of just being:

     WHO/WHAT the hell is this
     protoplasmic, gelatinous,
     fragile, and mortal thing
     programmed and named to be
     ricardo sánchez?    i cringe
in my fears (inwardly!)
while outwardly pose in guises
which assure me the timespace to survive
until my human frangibility can no longer hope
nor strive to continue surviving . . .

alleged poet, writer, ex-con, doctor of philosophy, scholar, lover, husband,
father, son, brother, friend, militant, activist, community organizer, and a
panoply of other labels,
i merely labor
to survive
just long enough
to learn and understand
how to live and love
whatever timespace i can share
with peoples and environments,

tired of hate and hurt, sickened by blood, gore and madness,
and angered by our callousness,
i seek to rectify
a past of wanton-ness
and find myself frustrated . . .

there does not exist
a way to quench my thirst

to love all that i wish to,

ay, each living thing i see
i want to understand and love,
each child, every person,
all differing lifeforms,

each form of land and cloud,
each tick or tock of time,
each salient word or thought,
each woman that i see,
each moment of awareness,
ay,
the process gains momentum,
and life continues on,
so onward shall i go
to quest and realize
that answers only live
within my struggle's process,
i live, i love, i sing,
i dance, i shout, i laugh,
i hurt, i joke, i hate,
i am a retinue of beings,
    a mirror for reality.


sonámbulo, no se puede
cantargritar, sólo
crear un dream
in the midst of realization . . .
2:00 a.m., tuesday, july 13, 76
   el chuco, te(de)jaslum


*
CDD = Chuco Del Diablo
GED = Gitano Erecting Daydreams (or high school equivalency?)
BL = Bato Loco
MD = Macho Dog (or Marihuana Doffer?)
PhD = Pinto highly Demented/Developed (or Doctor of Philosophy?)
SV = Se Vale
CS = Con Sapos (or Con Safos?)
PPJ = Poeta Pedagógico Jodido (or Pinche Pinto Jodido?)

   ps: pinto means ex-convict or convict! cabula means jive . . .

Josephine Saunders

(March 1972)

# THE CIRCLE AND THE QUESTION

All the invisible hands
are linked with each other to form
that invisible circle
out of which
arise such tangible things.

It is intimate here in the dark
with the snail in his house like a hat;
he too has joined hands;
and for this the stones have grown
arms, hands, fingers.—

Inside the circle, but not of it,
uninvolved,
I listen to the beauty
of the circular voices:

to the ambidextrous frog;

to the hung-up spider regaling
the shadow side of the mountain.

But I do not ask,
"Tell me everything! Tell me!" that
is neither my sign nor my right:

I have not wandered covetous
in a grove of arrows;

I have never thirsted after
either bird or stone.

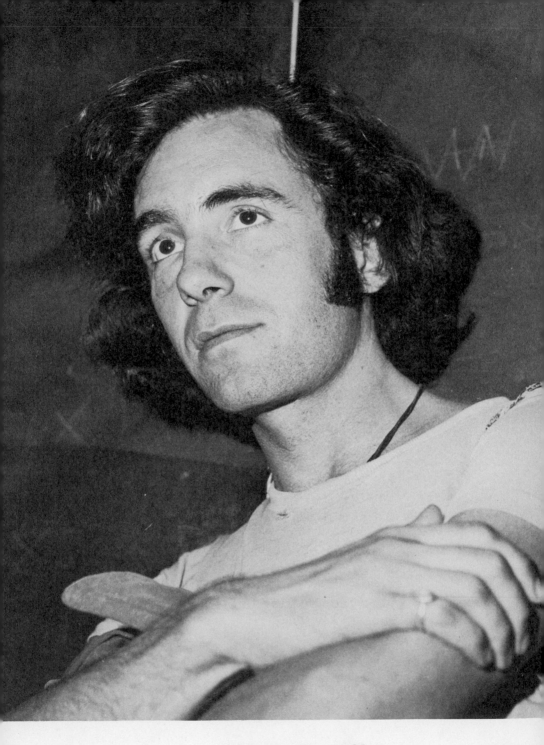

# Harris Schiff

(May 1975)

# IN THE HEART OF THE EMPIRE

IN THE HEART OF THE EMPIRE  the nightsounds
tingle the gyzmatic box        the sensor   in the giant sensorium
this comfort      now fleeting    &     not so fleeting
        now elusive
                                now found      now nowhere around
I am dreaming
                I'm not dreaming
                                        I wish I were dreaming


I am trapped in a geography of chemicals & I don't mind as long as
it don't hurt too much        & I don't know what to do about the pain
of my brother & sister creatures on this planet    or how to look them
in the eye    & have something to say besides    cry


        there are so many freaks            & yes


        there has been so much joy in all of us              especially
those soft come sleeps        & mother dreams      or the sunflower
                showers of radiation        & elation
        to be running over        earth's gentle tresses        hillsides


                        beneath sky
                                man
                                        pure sky
        which we come out of & return to
                                        like water back to water
        which is also alive
                        while in the street        the usual madmen
reflect the faces of the demons that made them mad
                                                which is to kill
                which is to be hungry
        which is to be insane in the wall of cacophonous sound
        & the steely brickbattered sootsky        reminder
    I'm not free                                I'm not free
                & no good    ever came out of the barrel of a gun
to splatter the flexing cerebrum
                                but watch out   for the jackboots   &
                                        the nightmare raiders

&  if it comes to that

                    would you want to be armed against all
possible assailants

               or rather   have none   & be   at ease
   so this is something we must all work towards

                           being high
  & unafraid        to shine it on
         like the cow mother who nourishes us
but she obliterates herself

              with heroin
     because of the dream that it will make you fine
        perpetrated by a liar    so subtle
   his face was hidden behind a beatific smile
   there is a promise        there is a promised land
          right in the body
but the land is overrun   by creatures who feel that someone
             must get the trains to

                   run on time

# Richard Shelton

(January 1970)

# NOTES TOWARD AN AUTOBIOGRAPHY:
## THE POET AT 41

### 1

don't expect smiles on all my faces
you won't have to look close
to see what I am
or what I want to become
or that I'm not becoming it

if you see me from a certain angle
on a better than average day
you will notice I am the other one
not the one you expected

it will appear that I have chosen
my shadow for its good behavior
and that I am bored by those women
whose bodies are all
they have to say to me

I will seduce
neither your wife nor your son
but I must tell you
that inside every thin poet
is a fat poet trying to get out

I do my best to keep him prisoner
don't offer me a second helping
of anything

### 2

when I remember where I came from
and how much I owe my sources
it is difficult to continue

I see my life flapping over the ground
the shadow of a dark wing
with no bird to guide it

but this too is self-indulgence
like guilt

it would be better to say
I will do what I can to entertain you
and for what I lack the courage to do
please forgive me

I would prefer to be completely honest
but then you would hate me
you see we all lie
for the same reasons

the hungry bat
in search of a vein is shameless
but more honest than any of us
can afford to be

3

living in the desert
has taught me to go inside myself
for shade

4

I am capable of giving rich gifts
when they are unexpected
but when someone asks me
for a match
I blush and fumble
embarrassed to give so much upon demand

5

I have a good marriage

a good marriage
is how we resolve the conflict
between who we want to go to bed with
and whose bed we want to wake up in

it's always a compromise

6

my old poems come back as strangers
and gradually I recognize

a gesture a worn-out coat
a tired smile

these were my companions
when I had no one else and they
were kind to me

how could I deny them now
when others speak only of their faults

7

showing the desert to a visitor
makes it real to me

when I say *this is an arroyo*
*this is a palo verde this is a saguaro*
these things exist
as if to support what I am saying
and the visitor believes me

but after he goes back
to wherever he came from
and I walk through the desert alone
I know the truth about this landscape
it does not exist
I dreamed it

8

the inevitable consequence
of a well-directed life is death
and the inevitable consequence
of a misdirected life
is also death

at night I keep telling myself
*go to sleep nobody is to blame*
*we are what we are*
*the world is what it is*

and eventually I go to sleep
but I never believe it

# Charles Simic

(March 1970)

# FURTHER ADVENTURES OF CHARLES SIMIC

Is Charles Simic afraid of death?
Yes, Charles Simic is afraid of death.

Does he pray for eternal life?
No, he carves a heart pierced by an arrow.

Tender as an onion in a skillet, he suffers
Chewing in earnest on his own brimstone.

And his conscience, does it bother him much?
He kisses his left hand which even under torture
    refuses to write anything.

The bones, ah the bones he feels them
As the convicts feel their handcuffs.

Does he lift his eyes humbly before the judges?
Her love was his judge, her hate the jury.

Gloominess' own conscript,
Son and Holy Ghost of his fears,
In a dark alley
His tongue will slash his throat.

## Gary Snyder
(February 1971)

## from MYTHS AND TEXTS

Spikes of new smell driven up nostrils
Expanding & deepening, ear-muscles
Straining and grasping the sounds
Mouth filled with bright fluid coldness
Tongue crushed by the weight of its flavours
      —the Nootka sold out for lemon drops
(What's this talk about not understanding!
     you're just a person who refuses to see.)

Poetry a riprap on the slick rock of metaphysics
"Put a Spanish halter on that whore of a mare
& I'll lead the bitch up any trail"

(how gentle! He should have whipped her first)

     the wind turns.
     a cold rain blows over the shale
     we sleep in the belly of a cloud
(you think sex art and travel are enough?
      you're a skinful of cowdung)

South of the Yellow River the Emperor Wu
Set the army horses free in the mountain pastures.
Set the Buffalo free on the Plain of the Peach Grove.
Chariots and armor were smeared with blood
    and put away.  They locked up
    the Arrows bag.
Smell of crushed spruce and burned snag-wood.
    remains of men,
Bone-chopped foul remains, thick stew
Food for crows—
    (blind, deaf, and dumb!
    shall we give him another chance?)
At Nyahaim-kuvara
Night has gone
Traveling to my land
    —that's a Mohave night

Our night too, you think brotherhood
Humanity & good intentions will stop it?
As long as you hesitate, no place to go.

Bluejay, out at the world's end
      perched, looked, & dashed
Through the crashing: his head is squashed.
      symplegades, the *mumonkwan.*
It's all vaginal dentata
      (Jump!)
"Leap through an Eagle's snapping beak"

Actaeon saw Dhyana in the Spring.

    it was nothing special
  misty rain on Mt. Baker,
      Neah Bay at low tide.

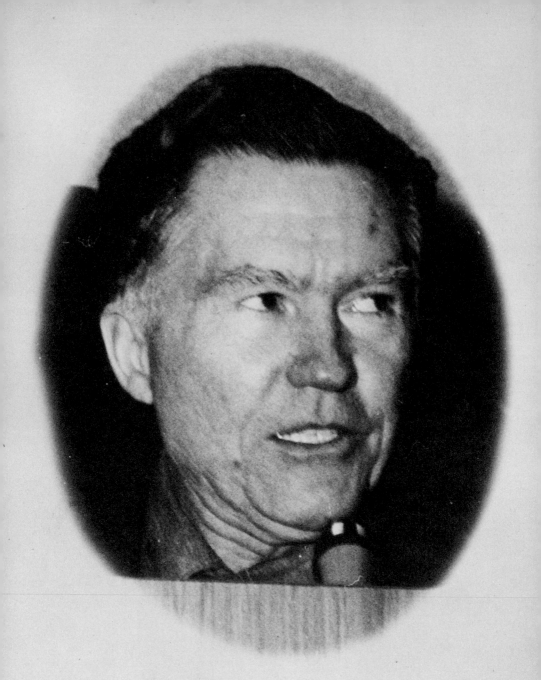

# William Stafford

(November 1971)

# CREDENTIALS

Few folk around here have
　　more leeries per post hoc
　　　　than I have.

They are more easy come
　　but also more easy go
　　　　than I am.

Or perhaps it's in the *propter*—
　　because they like to speak . . . .
　　　　I'm a speak-low doubter.

# Ruth Stephan

(April 1971)
deceased

# THE WIND

Leaves, wind-torn, sun-smoothed in passage,
hushed from tree speech, brown on the ground,
sigh against each other, no rage,
no doubt in changing. What is found,

Unfound, felt or unfelt blows by.
Winds rise, the air responds in song.
There is no ground without a sky,
no sky that does not have a song.

Softly desire, Love's wind-word,
stirs the laid leaves, is held and heard.


# SECOND WIND

Love's strength, like the tiger's smile,
springs from an invisible
impetuous, proud, wind-flipped guile,
lightning by name, yet lily-still.

In Autumn falls what is to fall—
the plum tree's promise, purpled plums,
rain, shadows, sighing leaves and all
things sun-heavy. Why ask what comes?

Love's legend moves with clouds, leaves, vows;
what was not there cannot fall now.

# Alan Stephens

(December 1964)

# SHORT WALK ALONE

Cool air just arriving; half moon
High, keen edged.
Air still and town still,
Lights on the mountain shine
As through punctures in the blackness,
Shapes like tiny explosions.

High, high in the eucalyptus—
Black bough tips in a black
Star-mild—a night-hawk cries out,
Twice, a gravelly scream,
That it's his darkness.
Coming back, catch a fragrance like cloves,
From some flowering bush or tree,
Near where the hawk claimed the dark.

Merely walking here seems
A kind of right spending
Of good, built up by the nature
Of things, by the race, by myself,
Brought within reach by the hang
Of the world as it has come
Quietly round, just here, just now.

# Pamela Stewart

(May 1976)

# SELF-PORTRAIT: WOMEN WITH CHILDREN:

The individual flakes, precise
As windows into conscience, are ignored
For a total sense of softening;
Our houses and the hills
With their stiff black trees rising
Behind all the scattered colors
Of children in the snow. So we think
Of interiors as contour, as a leg

That grows muscular and dark with bending
In the night. This last expression
Of a day
Says the past was not cruel
But an exciting in-between, a scarlet weather
We muffle the exactness of; the way
We drag our children
Into heavy clothes for entering winter.

We live
With this hazy version of ourselves
As charming figures
Turning down the sheets, but wish
We were perfectly beautiful
As often the children are
In sleep. Their startling scent
Is remote and sexual
Like the golden breasts dreamt of by a man
In his chair: the slow bodies

Pulling back and out of breath, escape
The keeping of it, the lunar form
Of what we haven't learned
But thought we had in memory
When, like now,
Last winter was filled with snow

And revolving silhouettes!

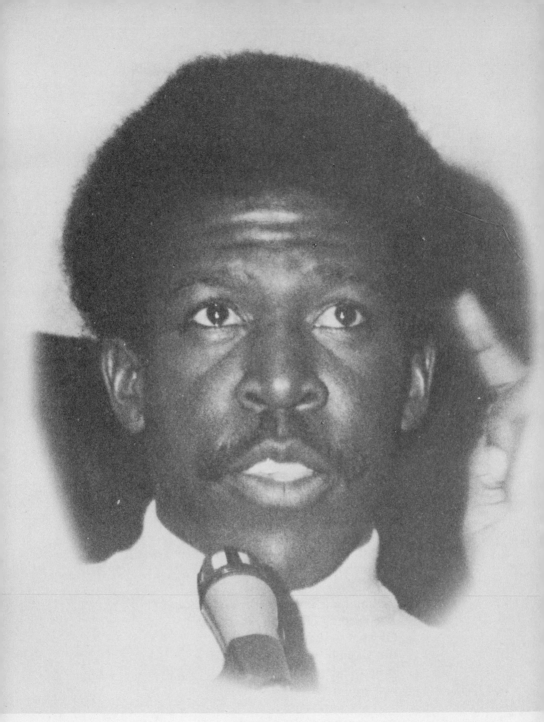

# Primus St. John
## (November 1971)

# THE CARPENTER

### 1

I look at my hands
In a dark hour.
They are my wife,
Another life,
Faunal,
Explicitly made.
I compare responsibility
To journey
They are pitch black
Whirling in the outside world
Left behind like a native—
Possessed.

### 2

We are older:
Toil is our long way
Back home.
It works.
Causes the space to beat
Like a heart.
Is is a part of the poem
That appears
And appears on its own.
It goes on
On its own,
Mystical as evil
But, it is called freedom.

### 3

I'm sorry:
I was telling you about my hands.
How well we are married.
It follows,
I recognize all truth
As some part of ten.
Spirit is my thumb,
Passionately.

Without thumb
I would be nothing.
I have met some who believe in reason.
They have had too much wine,
Confess cause and effect
It has been painful.

4

I told you it is unreasonable:
I guess I should say here,
I am your carpenter.
Ethically, dark wood
Is my life.
I could show you my story better,
Sanding,
Then when I speak
You would hear
    *Africa*
    *Africa*
One more thing, my love.
I have discovered in this dark wood
A skill you have called our loneliness.
I sand it down for you
Until our bodies fall off.

# Ruth Stone

(December 1965)

# RHYTHM

I am the drummer's daughter.
He beat time out of me.
Rat-a-tat-tat
Rat-a-tat-tat
In Norfolk on the sea.
Young he was and handsome.
A gambler, by G.
I was his first-born daughter.
He rolled the dice for me.
And down I dropped ripe as a plum
Out of my mama's belly.

Young he was and handsome
And he lived carelessly.
The sailors rolled him over
And took his green money.
My mama sewed his pockets up
But it didn't work, by G.
We were poor, my mama and I,
In Norfolk on the sea.
Boom, boom, rat-a-tat-tat
Down dropped another little brat
Out of my mama's belly.

I hardly saw my daddy,
His music set him free.
He slept in my mama's great big bed
And he smelled of strong whiskey.
My mama laughed and scolded
Happy as she could be.
Boom, boom, rat-a-tat-tat
Down dropped another little brat
Out of my mama's belly.

My daddy's dust is scattered.
My mama's salt as the sea.
And when I'm ready to lay me down
Here's what they'll say of me.
She is a drummer's daughter.
She learned what her Daddy taught her.

Never to drink cold water
And to keep her pockets free.
To beat time out of her heart
Or she must lose at the start
For, if she's a drummer's daughter,
She'll have to beat time, by G.

# Mark Strand

(May 1971)

# UNTITLED

He would look at the stars
And their distance confirmed what he felt
If there was order, then he was a part of it;
If there was choas, then it wasn't his fault . . .

# Robert Sward

(October 1965)

# THE 1950's

For the first time in 2000 years
one went 4 years to a University
without saying one true word
going to work for Hallmark Greeting cards
or the phone company
one knew something was at hand because things
became easy.
Poems arrived at one's door
in little four-line stanzas
Tin-Pan alley
people in college dormitories listening to Pat Boone

The 12-lb. baby is wearing
her white satin slippers.
She has a red dot
            on her nose.
Her eyes are blue.
She knows when she's getting
            what she wants.

Birds flutter and when they walk
they flutter too.

On some unanticipated astral plane,
in the midst of yoga,
the doctor makes a mental note to turn
his socks inside out to empty
out the sand before putting
them into the laundry bag.

He sees the cartoon strip *Nancy*,
old television re-runs.
A freshly cut pumpkin
with six legs like noodles
            dancing.

## May Swenson
### (February 1965)

# I LOOK AT AN OLD PHOTO OF MYSELF WITH LOVE

That I do bring myself to death
I do perceive,
but only now and then, like stars
and blindnesses between.
That I have brought myself to birth
I wish, and would believe,
to have deserved my innocence
before I earned its stain.

With youth's eyes I looked across
into my eyes of age.
When did I let a dot of death
impinge upon the edge
of irises undamaged,
that once were skies of truth?
Now I look with sullied eyes
into my eyes of youth
like a guilty lover
who has betrayed his oath.

And so I hang suspended
in the column of a well,
its wall my long pupil,
while the stars wheel,
my scope the slate lake
that I am swimmer in.
Into the mind's slit
I let death spill.

Yet, dilated now and then
out to the first rim,
I do rake immortal light
again from the birth room,
where my stare mates with its star.
Again, then, I begin.

# D.M. Thomas
(November 1971)

# DREAM

My woman said to me
I feel so guilty
at never knowing your father

      why don't you let him
      come and fetch me on sunday
      for the big easter tea at your house
      instead of you?

          And have him come early
          then he can sleep with me
          if you don't mind

      Mind! I was very please and excited
      easter day parties at our house
      are terribly grim with the dead
      still in their grave clothes & still dying
      & just a cup of potato wine

When I met him from the cemetery
it was wonderful
to see him so much better & younger
so wiry & healthy &
filthy dirty from work & his carroty
hairtufts I'd forgotten
making his whole body glow like an indian brave

      but when it came to it
      I didn't like to ask him
      if he'd fetch my woman

          because he'd forgotten the letter f
          & fourteen years of death
          makes driving strange & dangerous

      it might seem I was taking advantage
      I couldn't be open with him

and he
      humble as always     reticent
      he didn't want to seem pushing

# Tomas Tranströmer

(November 1975)

# GUARD DUTY

I am ordered out into a pile of stones,
like a noble corpse from the Iron Age.
The others may stay in the tent and sleep,
fanned out like spokes in a wheel.

In the tent presides the stove: a big snake
that has swallowed a gob of flame and hisses.
But it's quiet out here in the spring night
among cold stones waiting for dawn.

Here in the cold I begin to fly
like a shaman: I fly to her body,
the parts left white by the bathing suit—
we were in full sunlight, the moss was warm.

I brush near those warm moments,
but cannot stay there for long.
I am whistled back from the distance,
I crawl out among stones. Here and now.

Mission: to be where I am.
Also, in my silly and solemn role,
I am the place
where creation works on itself.

It dawns. The sparse tree trunks
have color now. The frostbitten forest
flowers send a search party
for anyone who's lost in the dark.

But to be where I am. And wait.
I am anxious, stubborn, confused.
Future events, they already exist!
I know it. They are out there:

a murmuring crowd outside the barricade.
They can only pass one by one.
They want to enter. Why? They come
one by one. I am the turnstile.

*translated by May Swenson*

# Diane Wakoski

(September 1971)

# I HAVE HAD TO LEARN TO LIVE WITH MY FACE

You see me alone tonight.
My face has betrayed me again,
    the garage mechanic who promises to fix my car
    and never does.

My face
that my friends tell me is so full of character;
my face
I have hated for so many years;
my face
I have made an angry contract to live with
though no one could love it;
my face that I wish you would bruise and batter
and destroy, napalm it, throw acid in it,
so that I might have another
or be rid of it at last.

I drag peacock feathers behind me
to erase the trail of the moon. Those tears
I shed for myself,
sometimes in anger.
There is no pretense in my life. The man who lives with me
must see something beautiful,

like a dark snake coming out of my mouth,
or love the tapestry of my actions, my life/this body, this
face, they have nothing to offer
but angry insistence, their presence.
I hate them,
want my life to be more.
Hate their shadow on even my words.

I sell my soul for good plumbing
and hot water,
                I tell everyone;
and my face is soft,
opal,
a feathering of snow
against the
        cold black leather coat
which is night.

You,
night,
my face against the chilly
expanse
of your back.
Learning to live with what you're born with
is the process,
the involvement
the making of a life.
And I have not learned happily
to live with my face,
that Diane which always looks better on film
than in life.
I sternly accept this plain face,
and hate every moment of that sternness.

I want to laugh at this ridiculous face
        of lemon rinds
        and vinegar cruets
        of unpaved roads
        and dusty file cabinets
        of the loneliness of Wall Street at night
        and the desert of school on a holiday
but I would have to laugh alone in a cold room
Prefer the anger
that at least for a moment gives me a proud profile.

Always, I've envied
        the rich
            the beautiful
                the talented
                    the go-getters
                        of the world. I've watched
myself
remain
alone
isolated
a fish that swam through the net
because I was too small
        but remained alone
        in deep water because others were caught
        taken away

266

It is so painful for me to think now,
to talk about this; I want to go to sleep and never wake up.
The only warmth I ever feel is wool covers on a bed.
But self-pity could trail us all, drag us around on the bottom of
shoes like squashed snails so that
we might never fight/and it is anger I want now, fury,
to direct at my face and its author,
to tell it how much I hate what it's done to me,
to contemptuously, sternly, brutally even, make it live with itself,
look at itself every day,
and remind itself
that reality is
learning to live with what you're born with,
noble to have been anything but defeated,
that pride and anger and silence will hold us above beauty,
though we bend down often with so much anguish for
a little beauty,
a word, like the blue night,
    the night of rings covering the floor and glinting
    into the fire, the water, the wet earth, the age of songs,
    guitars, angry busloads of etched tile faces, old gnarled
    tree trunks, anything with the beauty of wood, teak, lemon,
    cherry
I lost my children because I had no money, no husband,
I lost my husband because I was not beautiful,
I lost everything a woman needs, wants,
almost
before I became a woman,
my face shimmering and flat as the moon
with no features.

I look at pictures of myself as a child.
I looked lumpy, unformed, like a piece of dough,
and it has been my task as a human being
to carve out a mind, carve out a face,
carve out a shape with arms & legs, to put a voice inside,
and to make a person from a presence.
And I don't think I'm unique.
I think a thousand of you, at least, can look at those old photos,
reflect on your life
and see your own sculpture at work.

I have made my face as articulate as I can,
and it turns out to be a peculiar face with too much
bone in the bridge of the nose, small eyes, pale lashes,
thin lips, wide cheeks, a rocky chin,
But it's almost beautiful compared to the sodden mass of dough I
                            started out with.

I wonder how we learn to live
with our faces?
They must hide so much pain,
so many deep trenches of blood,
so much that would terrorize and drive others away, if they
could see it. The struggle to control it
articulates the face.
And what about those people
With elegant noses and rich lips?

What do they spend their lives struggling for?

Am I wrong I constantly ask myself
to value the struggle
more than the results?
Or only to accept a beautiful face
if it has been toiled for?

Tonight I move alone in my face;
want to forgive all the men whom I've loved
who've betrayed me.
After all, the great betrayer is that one I carry around each day,
which I sleep with at night. My own face,
angry building I've fought to restore
imbued with arrogance, pride, anger and scorn.
To love this face
would be to love a desert mountain,
a killer, rocky, water hard to find, no trees anywhere/
perhaps I do not expect anyone
to be strange enough to love it;
but you.

# David Rafael Wang

(June 1975)
deceased

# THE SELF-CONSCIOUS HORSE

I was born in the Year of the Horse
and when others started to neigh
I roared.

I have roared for forty-four years
and am king of the beasts
when my roar
scores knockouts
against the stalls.

## Larry Weirather

(June 1976)

# COMMUNION PORTRAIT IN OIL

## I

Like me are you still searching
For the Great American Epic?
Then simply rewrite *Moby Dick*.
Nothing has changed.
The name of the game is still oil.
Simply substitute petroleum for whale oil
And you have the same story:
Man creates his energy out of death.
Blackness yields to him his light.
The dark, dead whale bodies of oil
Used to feed the lamps of New Bedford.
Now black fossil fuel, death
Pumped or ripped from earth
Like strips of whale blubber
Light and heat the New World.
The earth becomes for us
The decapitated sperm whale's head,
A dead, cooling hulk awash
In the ocean void of space.
We dip our iron buckets into it,
Probing ever deeper to extract
The precious sperm to make us productive.
How ironic the word sperm.
All those oil wells simply go through
The sexless mechanics of sex,
A perversion of procreation—
Busily pumping away for all their worth.
The only issue or reproduction
Will come as death spewn
From the womb of the earth,
An abortion forced upward
By pumping seawater into the wells.
From the depths of the earth ocean
Of many layered rock and faults,
The black birth races upward, landward.
The oil knows nothing has changed.
It can still taste the salt
On its lips, heavy like blood,
Salty like blood, as it rises

From that deep, dark pelvic crush,
Feeling union with the traces
Of whale oil in those underground tides.
Man does not share in the communion
Where each partakes of the other.
Seamen cannot explain why
On some mysterious moonless nights
Oil in the storage tanks
Of tankers in the Middle East
Suddenly shifts its mass
As if huge flukes
Are rolling over in the hold.
Or a wildcatter cannot understand
Why he struck salt water
On sinking a dry well.
The oil waits patiently
For the day when a driller
Questions whether spots on his shirt
Are really oil or ages old whale blood.
Ahab's obsession has not lessened.

## II

Let me make another suggestion
For updating *Moby Dick*.
Change the setting from sea to land,
To the Great Permian Basin in Texas,
That seemingly measureless oil reservoir.
Just listen to the name—Permian.
It sounds like giant sperm whales,
Unseen leviathans, moving dimly down there
Through the basin's layered plankton gloom.
Place the setting in the heart of the basin
Where the oil to send man to the stars
Mixes with sulfur smelling of hell.
Place the setting in the heart of the basin
Near Midland, Texas—Midland,
Which symbolizes the center of anywhere
Just as "Pequod" translates as "a microcosm."
Just as few spouts are to be seen
At sea today, few spouts are seen
In the Permian oil fiels either.
The blowout of a well "coming in"

("Thar she blows"—whale or well)
Is as accidental now as a whale.
Engineers are fired for permitting blowouts.
There can be no waste
Though the soul dies.
Gone are the days when men stood
By the derricks as if they were masts,
Watching the wells spout like whales.
Yet the old pegleg will remains:
Out in the fields rides a roughneck,
A young Texas buck.  His name
Is Starbuck, a name that could
Only be produced in the Lone Star state
Of the mind, in Ahab's isolation.
He lives in a trailor court in Odessa
Not far from Midland.
He kills pale jackrabbits from his pickup
And rides it like a seasick altar.
He travels his women on back roads
And works on them without love
In the same motion as the pumping wells.
No one has told him he is an archetype.
No one has asked him
Why he pays for his beer at the bar
With doubloons crucified by nails,
Why he keelhauls the beer around his tongue
And logs another wail with his silence.

### III

Far out at sea a Russian whaler
From another Odessa or Perm
Fires an explosive charge
Into the head of a lolling fluked body.
The whale does not know it is protected
As it dives in death to reach
The permafrost currents of the depths.
It does not know the oil in its head
Will be used for a warhead
To arc the coldness of space.
Only whale oil can lubricate
some parts of a Russian ICBM,
Can be sensitive to baleen ballistics.

The parts are lovingly bathed
To produce death and light,
To play their part in a giant harpoon,
To make the horizon brighten and writhe
Like a stricken white whale on impact.
It is targeted for Texas.
Its brightness blinds.
It wishes to eat raw steak
Like Queequeg on the Texas prairie.
It wishes to stare on the white alkali
Of the Texas prairie as bleached whale bones.
Painted on its side like a code
Or a mysterious whale marking or wound
Inflicted by a tentacle in the deep
Is a lone red star that seeks communion
With the Lone Star State. Starbuck,
It wants you for its first mate.
From a distance the star looks strangely
Like a doubloon nailed to a silver mast.
The Russian tar knows none of this.
He simply coffins the whales
And throws his doubloons on the bar,
And like Starbuck
Lights up a cigarette,
Blowing upward a spout of smoke
That dissipates in the barroom light
In a vortex
Like the Pequod
Going under.

# Richard Wilbur
(April 1973)

# PICCOLA COMMEDIA

He is no one I really know,
The sun-charred, gaunt young man
By the highway's edge in Kansas
Thirty-odd years ago.

On a tourist-cabin veranda
Two middle-aged women sat;
One, in a white dress, fat,
With a rattling glass in her hand,

Called, "Son, don't you feel the heat?
Get up here into the shade."
Like a good boy, I obeyed,
And was given a crate for a seat

And an Orange Crush and gin.
"This state," she said, "is hell."
Her thin friend cackled, "Well, dear,
You've gotta fight sin with sin."

"No harm in a drink; my stars!"
Said the fat one, jerking her head.
"And I'll take no lip from Ed,
Him with his damn cigars."

Laughter.  A combine whined
On past, and dry grass bent
In the backwash; liquor went
Like an ice-pick into my mind.

Beneath her skirt I spied
Two sea-cows on a floe.
"Go talk to Mary Jo, son
She's reading a book inside."

As I gangled in at the door
A pink girl, curled in a chair,
Looked up with an ingénue stare.
*Screenland* lay on the floor.

Amazed by her starlet's pout
And the way her eyebrows arched,
I felt both drowned and parched.
Desire leapt up like a trout.

"Hello," she said, and her gum
Gave a calculating crack.
At once, from the lightless back
Of the room there came the grumble

Of someone's heaving from bed,
A Zippo's click and flare,
Then, more and more apparent,
The shuffling form of Ed,

Who neither looked nor spoke
But moved in profile by,
Blinking one gelid eye
In his elected smoke.

This is something I've never told,
And some of it I forget.
But the heat! I can feel it yet,
And that conniving cold.

# Peter Wild

(September 1972)

# SILVER

Who would want silver on the table?
the Lone Ranger wouldn't, he would
send him down the hill to the corral
to help the wild pigs break apart the blocks
of hay with their noses, paw into them
for the china with its willows
eaten to a lace by the bridge.
sitting on a hill with his napkin
spread on the curve of the earth, troubled
by the wind he might think that it
would blow the crumbs away all at once
in a gust, a shining fist that dipped
over the badlands, along the contours of the prairie,
rushed into the cave like a blast
salting it, so that arriving days later
in need of ammunition, pursued
by the fat sheriff with twisted logic,
who loves his children, the priest
shuffles out ashamed, hands spread
and says there isn't any, that at night
he heard the glowing perpetual vein
leap out of its crib, fly like a mad patient
down the narrowing tunnel to the lake
deep in the source of the earth
where no man can fit. for the women he
keeps his burnt flint jaw scraped
free of sweat; and that is why
approaching gutted or abandoned houses
he treads like a boy having forgotten
he once stole apples there, confident
in the charm of the invisible horse between his legs
ready to spin him off at the touch of a spur,
turns away at the croaking of
a coyote, his friend with his hand
over his mouth behind the charred bannisters,
in mufti rides over to the widow's place, wad of dry algae
that lurches toward him from her shack, arms spread, white
hair wild around the sun of her face,
bathes his wounds, serves him marmalade.

# C.K. Williams
(February 1970)

# SPIT

*... then the son of the 'superior race' began to spit into the Rabbi's
mouth so that the Rabbi could continue to spit on the Torah ...*

The Black Book

After this much time, it's still impossible. The SS man with his stiff hair
    and his uniform;
the Rabbi, probably in a torn overcoat, probably with a stained beard the
    other would be clutching;
the Torah, God's word, on the altar, the letters blurring under the
    blended phlegm;
the Rabbi's parched mouth, the SS man perfectly absorbed, obsessed with
    perfect humiliation.
So many years and what is there to say still about the soldiers waiting
    impatiently in the snow,
about the one stamping his feet, thinking, "Kill him! Get it over with!"
while back there the lips of the Rabbi and the other would have brushed
and if time had stopped like that you would have thought they were lovers,
so lightly kissing, the sharp, luger hand under the dear chin,
the eyes furled slightly and then when it started again the eyelashes of both
    of them
shyly fluttering as wonderfully as the pulse of a baby.
Maybe we don't have to speak of it at all, it's still the same.
War, that happens and stops happening but is always somehow right there,
    twisting and hardening us;
then what we make of God—words, spit, degradation, murder, shame;
    every conceivable torment.
All these ways to live that have something to do with how we live
and that we're almost ashamed to use as metaphors for what goes on in us
but that we do anyway, so that love is battle and we watch ourselves in love
become maddened with pride and incompletion, and God is what it is
    when we're alone
wrestling with solitude and everything speaking in our souls turns against
    us like his fury,
and just facing another person, there is so much terror and hatred that yes,
spitting in someone's mouth, trying to make him defile his own meaning,
would signify the struggle to survive each other and what we'll enact to
    accomplish it.

There's another legend.
It's about Moses, that when they first brought him as a child before
    Pharoah,
the king tested him by putting a diamond and a live coal in front of him
and Moses picked up the red ember and popped it into his mouth
so for the rest of his life he was tongue-tied and Aaron had to speak for him.
I wonder what his scarred tongue must have felt like in his mouth:
it must have been like always carrying something there that weighed too
    much,
something leathery and dead whose greatest gravity was to loll out like an
    ox's,
and when it moved, it must have been like a thick embryo slowly coming
    alive,
butting itself against the inner sides of his teeth and cheeks.
And when God burned in the bush, how could he not cleave to him?
How could he not know that all of us were on fire and that every word we
    said would burn forever,
in pain, unquenchably, and that God knew it, too, and would say nothing
    Himself ever again beyond this,
ever, but would only live in the flesh that we use like firewood,
in all the caves of the body, the gut cave, the speech cave:
He would slobber and howl like something just barely a man that beats
    itself again and again onto the dark,
moist walls away from the light, away from whatever would be light for
    this last eternity.
"Now therefore go," He said, "and I will be with thy mouth."

# Keith Wilson

(November 1969)

# THE TOUCH OF MOONLIGHT

My male ancestors
prowled this land
like heavy mountain
cats spewing their
hatred and their life
dropping spoor, flicking
tail, a howl in their chests
for the darkness, the chipped
winds of the highroad valleys

—my dad was tailed by
a puma all the way back
from some girl's house. He
forgets her name, but he went
back the next night, quick
-shadowed as any cat, its
cries like a woman's cries
breaking through the shafts
of moonlight

I, I walk the high thin
fences, domesticated,
dig my claws in rotten
wood and feel my belly
rock from side to side
as the door opens, yellow
street light!  and out
into a night crisp with
exhaust smoke and pretence

I, I am a fatcat and walk
the slender fences of a city
remembering woods

                    the touch
of moonlight on my eyes, the
touch of moonlight

# James Wright

(February 1973)

# THE JEWEL

There is this cave
In the air behind my body
That nobody is going to touch:
A cloister, a silence
Closing around a blossom of fire.
When I stand upright in the wind,
My bones turn to dark emeralds.

# Marguerite Young
(February 1966)

# THE PROCESS

O, could clock hands be moved in either way
And process seem, as it should be simply, reversible,
Yet would we mistrust that Lazarus of octopus and sea-
Lilies evolving then toward mute infantile,

O, woeful then in the sea! nor aged fox's cracked microscosm
Of the golden grapes upon the golden bough,
For there would be no retardation of that early theme
Wherein he questioned the validity of all.

And when clouded leopards leap, leap and love
How woeful then, the ever brightening eye
Could God and ourselves as functioning retrieve;
For all our deaths would be our first birthday,

Ourselves, and the moose, and lotus buds in that cold,
                                                    dark river,
Ourselves, and the ermine whitening in the white snow
Hastening harrowed. How woeful then, the bright electric
    hairs
And the vacancy of every brow,

For when toward the seed ovule would recede each green
    tree
And yesterday would be today, for all our sakes,
Yet would we persist in elegy,
Lament each one the rosebud of his lip,

The womb as tomb, and foetus coiled no more to flower,
And the annihilation of our strange sorrowing
When that tomorrow of a never doubted hour
Is time before the first angel falling.

How wasted then, the flesh made rounded and firm
And winging toward childhood, every snow-greaved swan
Till brief as snow in summer
Swan, there's none

293

Nor timeless brightness ours; for carried to a just terminus
That reason seems an ever tolling bell;
And this, the loud tumult of the whirling geese,
And our mischance may yet be possible.

# Paul Zimmer
## (February 1971)

# ZIMMER IN WINTER

I am always happiest in winter.
Though I begin by
Striding beneath resolute skies,
Furrowing the drifts toward some violence,
I always end in a joyful place.

In winter my heart is sound
As a frozen stone, and my teeth
Are resonant icicles.
                        In winter
The trees have already dropped
Their easy parts upon my mind.

My left eye rising cold in the mountains,
My right eye slipping beneath ice in the river,
I come to a place
Where the coldest crystals shine the most,
Where my hair clings softly to the twig mats
And all my holes contain white rabbits.

Twenty years ago . . .
Student newspaper reporter-photographer LaVerne Harrell interviews poet Robert
Peter Tristram Coffin at T.W.U., Denton, Texas. Photo by Robbie Stanley.

Today . . .
LaVerne Harrell Clark and L.D. Clark at Writer's Conference, Santa Fe, New
Mexico. Photo by James Ralph Johnson.

LaVerne Harrell Clark, author, photographer, and lecturer, was born in Smithville, Texas, a "Depression baby," and was educated at the Texas Woman's University, where in 1973 she was named a Distinguished Alumna; at Columbia University; and at the University of Arizona. After working for a year as a newspaper reporter in Fort Worth, and for several years at various publishers' in New York City, she became the first Director of the University of Arizona Poetry Center (1962-'66). Since 1966, she has devoted her time to her own writings, photography, and to traveling extensively in Europe (especially Spain), Mexico, and among Southwestern American Indians, where she has conducted in-depth folklore field research, initially on a grant from the American Philosophical Society.

Author of the award-winning paperback *They Sang For Horses* (University of Arizona Press, 1971), Clark has published numerous articles on Navajo, Apache, Hopi, and Pueblo Indians, as well as on the Sioux and Cheyenne related to Mari Sandoz' life and works. Many contain her own photos. Additionally she has written and photographed entirely the following books: *Revisiting The Plains Indian Country of Mari Sandoz* (Blue Cloud Chapbooks, 1977), and *Focus 101* (Heidelberg Graphics, 1979), which serves as an illustrated biographical companion to *The Face of Poetry*. More recently she has been reading her current fiction on tour and at writers' conferences. It appears in *Pawn Review, Texas Quarterly, Nitty-Gritty,* and is anthologized in *Southwest* (1977), edited by Karl and Jane Kopp and Bart Lanier Stafford III.

Clark's photos related to D.H. Lawrence's travels have illustrated various articles and notably these books by her husband, novelist-literary critic L.D. Clark: *Dark Night of The Body* (University of Texas Press, 1964), and the forthcoming *The Minoan Distance* (University of Arizona Press). The winner of nine nationally prestigious awards for her writings, photography and lectures—among them the First Place International Folklore Prize of the University of Chicago (1967)—has lived most of her life in the Southwest, especially at her present home in Tucson, where her husband is a Professor of English at the University of Arizona.

Co-editor Mary MacArthur, designer and publisher of the first edition of *The Face of Poetry*, Gallimaufry Press, 1977. Photo by Ted Merrill.

## ABOUT CO-EDITOR MARY MacARTHUR

In January 1979 Mary MacArthur was appointed Assistant Director of the Literature Program of the National Endowment for the Arts. She then left her position as editor and publisher of Gallimaufry Press and *Gallimaufry Journal*, which she founded in 1973.

She was a founding member of the Board of the Writer's Center at Glen Echo, Maryland, where she continued to serve on the Board of Directors until January 1979. She was a member of the Poetry Advisory Committee of the Folger Shakespeare Library in Washington, D.C., and a member of the Northern Area Arts Advisory Panel of the Virginia Commission on the Arts and Humanities.

A former resident of San Francisco, Ms. MacArthur worked at the West Coast Print Center and was a Director and founding Member of the Small Press Center, a non-profit literary project. In addition, Ms. MacArthur served for two years on the Board of Directors of the Committee of Small Magazines, Editors and Publishers (COSMEP).

She currently resides in Washington, D.C., with her husband, Richard Grossman, and her five-year old daughter, Alyssa.

Poets anthologized in *The Face of Poetry* are listed in

## FOCUS 101

An Illustrated Biography of 101 Poets of the 60's & the 70's
Photographs, text and editing by LaVerne Harrell Clark
(Heidelberg Graphics, Chico, CA 95927, 1979; ISBN 0-918606-03-9
$7.95 + $1.00 shipping)

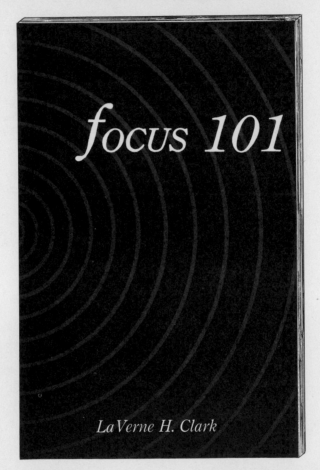

"...A companion piece to *The Face of Poetry*, it contains short
biographies and photographs of 101 leading poets of the 60's
and 70's...a unique book that will be of value to every reader
of modern poetry...I highly recommend *Focus 101* by LaVerne
Harrell Clark."

—Bart Lanier Stafford III
*"The Book Shelf,"* **El Paso**